FRUIT

FRUIT

RECIPES THAT CELEBRATE NATURE

BERNADETTE WÖRNDL
PHOTOGRAPHY BY GUNDA DITTRICH

For Anton – the apple of my eye.

RHUBARB –
FRUIT OR VEGETABLE?

A PREFACE

During my research for this book, I often came up against the question of whether rhubarb is actually considered a vegetable, even though, broadly speaking, it belongs to the fruit family. Should rhubarb, therefore, be in this book?

Fruits in the general sense are primarily still fruits in the botanical sense – that is, the part of the plant that emerges from the flowers. Vegetables comprise all the other possible edible plant parts – flowers (artichokes), leaves (spinach), tubers (potatoes) or stems (asparagus). With rhubarb, only the leaf stem (petiole) of the plant is used (the leaves are unusable because of their high oxalic acid content). From this, it is quite clear that rhubarb is actually a vegetable, while tomatoes and zucchini (courgettes) are, botanically speaking, actually fruit.

Rather, than let scientific reasons make the decision, I wanted to follow my own taste and cooking traditions. Our dietary habits play a part in whether we use a foodstuff as a fruit or a vegetable: fruits we generally eat raw; vegetables usually cooked. And from fruit we expect a certain sugar content and a sweet taste. Rhubarb only began to be used as a 'fruit' when sugar became affordable and it could be eaten as a dessert, and I generally use the pink stalks for sweet rather than savoury dishes. Its sourness harmonises especially well with strawberries. How clever of nature to let these ripen at the same time for a brief moment, as the first offering of spring. Or just-stewed rhubarb with yoghurt – so pure and simple – it needs nothing else. Equally, lamb in milk with rhubarb is also in no way to be disregarded. Briefly fried with olive oil, butter, thyme, salt, pepper and dessert wine, rhubarb also makes a tart accompaniment for poultry, pork or fish that's really worth trying. But enough about rhubarb.

TOMATO *and* MELON

In contrast, the tomato is usually treated as a vegetable – including by me. Nevertheless, you could easily include fully ripe tomatoes in a summer fruit salad or serve cherry tomatoes stewed in vanilla syrup with ice cream.

Melon is also, botanically speaking, a fruit. Most people value it for its sweetness, but it can be used just as well in savoury dishes. This is one reason why it has earned its place in this book.

REGION *and* SEASON

Apart from botanical and cultural criteria, another factor influenced my choice of which fruits to include in this book: provenance. I restricted myself to local fruit because it's very important to me to cook with regional and seasonal ingredients – always starting with fresh fruit harvested in its fully ripe splendour. That way, sufficient variety on the plate is guaranteed. It was only the citrus fruits I couldn't leave out entirely, because without lemons and oranges my cooking wouldn't be complete. And lemons can also be successfully grown in a winter garden or greenhouse in cooler climates.

Dried fruits are also a great way to integrate different sorts of fruit into meals, especially in winter, when besides apples and oranges there is very little fresh fruit. I've allowed myself here to look beyond the rim of the plate and use dried fruits such as dates or barberries. In that way, fruit accompanies us throughout the year and helps to make our mealtimes varied.

The seasonal key in the recipes can shift somewhat or change each year, depending on the weather and the

region, but it always refers to the particular fruit that was used. Those in the Dried Fruit chapter can, of course, be cooked year-round, so here I've placed the emphasis on the season in which the accompanying vegetables appear. Apart from the blood orange recipes, the dishes in the citrus fruit section can, too, be made throughout the year. Even though the actual season for these fruits is autumn/winter, our body tells us that ceviche or citrus sorbet tastes much better in summer and does us good. Or that the still teeny-tiny beetroot (beets) that grow first each year, along with their leaves, make a salad with citrus fruits and avocado even more delicate. And so here an exception to the seasonal calendar is allowed.

STORING and PRESERVING
Some fruit, such as apples, can be stored for months at cellar temperature (10–13°C/50–55°F). Freshly picked strawberries, however, usually don't even last the afternoon and need to be used straight away. In general, wild strawberries, which we pick in Europe on the edge of the forest, should simply end up in the mouth and as soon as possible.

Preserving fruits in syrup, pickled or salted is one of the best methods to extend their storage life, and to also enjoy fruit outside harvest time. Each year in my kitchen, I look forward to filling lots of small jars with marmalades, jams (jellies), stewed fruit, chutneys and syrups. That way you can be sure, one glooomy winter's morning, of bringing back a few rays of sunlight with some spoonfuls of stewed apricots over your breakfast muesli. Or you can perfect a slice of toast spread with cream cheese by crowning it with fig chutney. Or indulge in a raw winter salad lifted with the sweet and sour of raspberry vinegar. And the best thing: a jar of home-preserved fruit always makes the most beautiful present next time you're invited to someone's house!

RECIPES from A to Z
The recipes in this book are organised from A to Z and each chapter opens with an image of whole fruit as a still life. A small symbol above each recipe reveals the season or seasons of the fruit used.

When writing the recipes, it was important to me not to lose sight of the classics and simple desserts. Because fruit, simply on its own and fully ripe is, of course, already a dessert. When I was with Alice Waters at Chez Panisse, a small bowl of fresh seasonal fruit was always offered at the end of a meal, often studded with dried or candied fruits. I fell in undying love with this simple way of celebrating fruits and their seasons. By the same token, I've also written recipes that feature more complex dishes, or reinterpreted creations I've come across in my travels or through talking to people. This way of assembling ingredients in a recipe is an important component of my cooking style.

And so the recipes range, from extremely simple dishes that rely on the quality of their few ingredients, through to jars full of preserved pure fruit and extravagant, previously uncelebrated combinations.

SWEET, SOUR *and* SALTY

Recipes with fruit traditionally move up and down, back
and forth on the scale from sweet via sour to salty. Think
of classics, such as prosciutto and melon, berries with
game or poultry and jam (jelly) with cheese.

Indian curries and African stews, but above all
Californian cuisine, prove that the sweetness or sourness
of fruit can tease special tastes out of a savoury dish.
In this way, new and interesting taste experiences and
a diversity of possible combinations open up.

FLEXIBILITY AND SERVES

As with herbs and vegetables, fruit should be washed
thoroughly before use to remove any dirt and
possible bacteria.

The recipes are generally designed to serve four people,
unless an entrée is served as a main or vice versa. With
cakes, chutneys and ice cream, there can sometimes
be enough leftover for a second helping or leftovers for
the next day. The pleasure of repeating a good meal is
usually enormous, and many dishes taste even better the
day after, making an opulent meal of leftovers.

It's also by all means allowed – no, I actually insist on
it – to change the quantities or even the ingredients
according to personal tastes, because that way each dish
becomes a completely personal banquet. I'd really love
to write my recipes only with descriptions like 'a handful
of', 'a dash of', 'a splash of this' and 'a touch of that',
but that's of course not possible. I want to urge you,
however, to trust yourself more in the kitchen,
to try things out, to modify recipes whether by desire or
whim, to transform them according to season or region,
to interpret them anew, possibly even to fail and to learn
from it! When you succeed, you discover new tastes and
you'll never become bored.

I finish writing this book in a country house in Apulia,
Italy. My desire for a creamy clafoutis, like the one I ate at
breakfast yesterday and described in the Cherries chapter,
begins to grow. I think of a link with the fresh apricots
that I bought this morning at the market and that are
in season at the moment, and in my head I start to mix
the dough with a spoon in a bowl: eggs, sugar, milk, just
a little flour. A piece of ricotta left over from breakfast,
along with the fresh zest of a lemon from the tree in the
garden and a few rosemary sprigs also make their way
into the dough – that surely can't hurt. There's no oven,
but I will try to use the remaining heat from the open
barbecue. After the first minute it's clear that the heat is
too high, and the clafoutis will be too dark in the middle.
And so I quickly put a pan under it and cover everything
with a second pan so that the top will also cook through.

It works – the smoky aroma of the barbecue goes
wonderfully well with the sweet and sour taste of the
apricots, the ricotta gives it creaminess and structure, and
the rosemary and lemon enhance the flavour. Tomorrow
evening I will carefully use the remaining heat again, and
instead of apricots I will use fresh figs from the garden.
Then it occurs to me – a savoury version, with prosciutto,
buffalo mozzarella and a little pecorino in the dough,
cooked in an earthenware pot, would make a beautiful
antipasto.

Long live the beauty of diversity!

CONTENTS

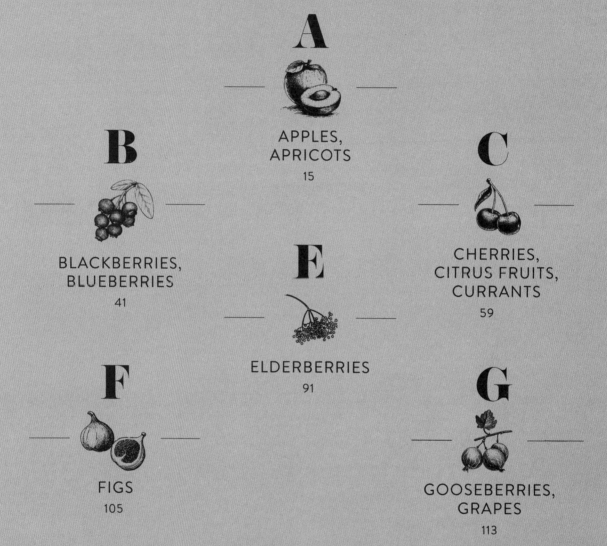

CONTENTS

A

APPLES, APRICOTS

BIRCHER MUESLI WITH GRATED APPLE, PEPITAS, YOGHURT AND FRESH GRAPES

*My favourite breakfast. It easily lends itself to seasonal combinations
using different grains, seeds and nuts or fruits.
A grated apple always makes an appearance, though.*

2 apples
1 handful walnuts
100 g (3½ oz / 1 cup) rolled (porridge) oats
2 tablespoons linseeds (flax seeds), roughly crushed
2 teaspoons wheat bran
2 tablespoons pepitas (pumpkin seeds)
150 ml (5 fl oz) milk
300 g (10½ oz) yoghurt
pinch of salt
small handful shelled pistachios
small handful grapes
honey, for drizzling

Coarsely grate one of the apples and roughly chop the walnuts. Place in a
bowl and add the oats, linseeds, wheat bran, pepitas, milk, 200 g (7 oz) of
the yoghurt and the salt. Stir well to combine, then cover and refrigerate
overnight to soak.

The next day, roughly chop the pistachios and coarsely grate the second
apple. Finely slice two grapes. Serve the muesli in shallow bowls and top with
the apple, remaining yoghurt, grapes, pistachios and a drizzle of honey.

BAKED APPLES
WITH VANILLA SAUCE

A wonderful way to use up left-over fruit bread, biscuits (cookies), gingerbread and cake, nuts or dried fruits.
The combination of apple, butter, sugar and cinnamon is one of the best there is.

Baked apples
50 g (1¾ oz) butter
4 apples
2 slices fruit bread or fruit cake
2 tablespoons walnuts or almonds
2 tablespoons dried fruit
(e.g. figs, dates, raisins, prunes,
apricots)

4–5 pieces candied lemon peel
(page 77) or candied orange peel
1 tablespoon honey
1 teaspoon cranberry jam (jelly)*
½ teaspoon ground cinnamon
pinch of salt
1 teaspoon soft brown sugar
100 ml (3½ fl oz) apple juice

Vanilla sauce
1 vanilla bean
400 ml (13½ fl oz) milk
60 g (2 oz) caster (superfine) sugar
2 egg yolks, lightly beaten
1 tablespoon cornflour (cornstarch)

Preheat the oven to 200°C (400°F) (conventional). For the baked apples, grease a baking dish with half the butter. Core the apples, reserving the apple tops, and scoop out about one-third of the apple flesh. Place the hollowed apples in the prepared dish. Dice the scooped-out apple and fruit bread or cake, and finely chop the walnuts or almonds, dried fruit and citrus peel. Place everything in a bowl, then stir in the honey, jam, cinnamon and salt. Fill the apples with this mixture and position the apple tops on top.

Cut the remaining butter into small pieces. Sprinkle the apples with the brown sugar and dot them with the butter. Pour over the apple juice and bake for 30–35 minutes, until soft and cooked through.

For the vanilla sauce, split the vanilla bean lengthways, scrape out the seeds and place both the bean and the seeds in a small saucepan, along with the milk. Add the sugar and egg yolks, and heat gently, stirring. Mix the cornflour with a little cold water until you have a smooth paste, then add to the milk and bring to the boil, stirring constantly, until thickened. Remove the vanilla bean, then pour the sauce into a serving jug and serve alongside the baked apples.

---

*   To make cranberry jam (jelly), bring 1 kg (2 lb 3 oz) cranberries, 50 ml (1¾ fl oz) water and 500 g (1 lb 2 oz) jam (jelly) sugar to the boil. Cook, stirring constantly, for 6–8 minutes. Allow to cool to room temperature, then store in sterilised jars. The jam will keep for 1 year.

GRANDMA'S
APPLE STRUDEL

It's no secret that I was rolling out strudel pastry with my grandmother at the age of three. On the farm we were surrounded by many varieties of apple trees, so apple cakes, apple strudels, apple sauce, stewed apples or baked apple slices were commonplace at home.

Strudel pastry
200 g (7 oz/1⅓ cups) plain (all-purpose) flour, plus extra for dusting
pinch of salt
2 tablespoons oil, plus extra for rubbing
110 ml (4 fl oz) lukewarm water

Filling
10–12 apples
½ teaspoon grated lemon zest
juice of 1 lemon
scraped seeds of ½ vanilla bean
60–70 g (2–2½ oz) caster (superfine) sugar

50–60 g (1¾–2 oz) raisins
4 teaspoons rum
120 g (4½ oz) butter
120 g (4½ oz) breadcrumbs
1 teaspoon ground cinnamon

Preheat the oven to 180°C (350°F) (conventional). For the strudel pastry, combine the flour, salt, oil and lukewarm water in a large bowl, and combine to form a smooth, elastic dough. Rub the dough with a few extra drops of oil, then cover and leave to rest at room temperature for 30 minutes.

For the filling, peel the apples, cut into quarters and remove the core. (Retain the peel and cores for another use.*) Slice the apples, not too thinly, and place in a large bowl with the lemon zest and juice, vanilla seeds, 30 g (1 oz) of the sugar, and the raisins and rum.

Dust a large tea towel (dish towel) evenly with flour. Using a rolling pin, roll out the strudel pastry on the tea towel as thinly as possible. Place your hands under the pastry, palms down, and gently stretch the pastry thinner and thinner with the backs of your hands, working from the centre outwards. Keep going until you can see the tea towel underneath. Don't worry if the pastry tears a little; a few small holes are fine.

Melt half the butter in a frying pan with the breadcrumbs and toast until golden brown. Mix in the cinnamon and remaining sugar. Melt the remaining butter separately and allow to cool a little. Brush the strudel dough with 3 tablespoons of the melted butter. Scatter the breadcrumb mixture over the dough, leaving a 5 cm (2 in) border. Top with the apple slices.

Fold the border over the filling then, using the tea towel to assist you, gently roll up the strudel and slide, seam side down, onto a large baking tray lined with baking paper. Brush with the remaining melted butter and bake for 35–40 minutes, until golden brown. Serve lukewarm or completely cooled.

---

* Make a syrup with the apple peel and cores by boiling them with 500 ml (17 fl oz/2 cups) naturally cloudy apple juice for 30–40 minutes. Strain and use in glazes, cocktails or as a sweet addition to porridge and salad dressings.

APPLE STRUDEL
WITH QUARK SHORTCRUST PASTRY

*Here is another version of apple strudel, which we call 'apfelschaling'. My grandpa was always
very proud of it, because we used his own wine from Lower Austria in the dough.*

Pastry
250 g (9 oz) plain (all-purpose) flour,
plus extra for dusting
200 g (7 oz) cold butter, cut into cubes
250 g (9 oz) quark
1 egg yolk
2 tablespoons white wine
pinch of salt

Filling
6–7 large apples
½ teaspoon finely grated lemon zest
juice of 1 lemon
1 teaspoon ground cinnamon
3–4 tablespoons caster (superfine) sugar
1 handful raisins (optional)

For brushing
1 egg white, lightly beaten

Using your fingertips, mix the flour with the butter in a
large bowl, until the mixture resembles breadcrumbs.
Add the quark, egg yolk, wine and salt and quickly
knead to a smooth dough. Wrap in plastic wrap and
leave to rest in a cool place for 1 hour.

Preheat the oven to 200°C (400°F) (conventional). Line
a large baking sheet with baking paper. Peel the apples,
cut into quarters and remove the cores. (Retain the
apple peel and cores for another use; see * opposite.)
Slice the apples, not too thinly, and place in a bowl
with the lemon zest and juice, cinnamon, sugar and
raisins, if using.

On a lightly floured work surface, roll the dough out
to 5–8 mm (¼ in) thick, then transfer to the prepared
baking sheet – it's fine if the edges hang over the sides
of the baking sheet. Spread the apple slices over the
middle, leaving a 3–4 cm (1¼–1½ in) border. Brush
the edges of the dough with the egg white. Fold in the
edges of the dough, then fold in the right third of the
strudel. Now fold the left third over the top. Brush the
strudel with egg white and bake for 30–40 minutes,
until crisp and cooked through.

Allow to cool completely or serve lukewarm.

ARCTIC CHAR ON APPLE KRAUT
WITH SEMOLINA DUMPLINGS

A combination I love, and one that blew me away iwhen I first tasted it in Alsace. There it's served with fried sausage and roast pork belly, but in this recipe I decided to focus on the fish and add a hint of pancetta.

Apple kraut	100 ml (3½ fl oz) white wine	1 tablespoon icing	100 g (3½ oz) semolina
2 French shallots	100 ml (3½ fl oz) vegetable	(confectioners') sugar	2 eggs
1 tablespoon clarified butter	stock or water	50 ml (1¾ fl oz) apple juice	
2–3 thyme sprigs	200 g (7 ȯz) sauerkraut		*Arctic char*
1 strip lemon zest	2 tablespoons crème fraîche	*Semolina dumplings*	2 × 200 g (7 oz) Arctic char
2 bay leaves	salt and freshly ground	250 ml (8½ fl oz / 1 cup)	fillets or similar
3 juniper berries	black pepper, to taste	milk	1 teaspoon butter
1 clove		50 g (1¾ oz) butter	4 thin slices pancetta
2–3 apples	*Caramelised apple*	good pinch of salt	2 thyme sprigs
1 teaspoon icing	2–3 apples	good pinch of freshly grated	1 teaspoon capers, rinsed
(confectioners') sugar	1 teaspoon butter	nutmeg	and squeezed dry

For the apple kraut, peel and halve the shallots, then cut into thin wedges. Heat the clarified butter in a frying pan, add the shallot and cook until transparent. Pick the thyme leaves and add to the pan, along with the lemon zest, bay leaves, juniper berries and clove. Cook until aromatic. Peel the apples, cut into quarters and remove the cores. Cut the apple into slices, then add to the pan and cook until soft. Add the sugar and caramelise, then deglaze the pan with the wine and stock. Add the sauerkraut with its liquid. Boil the apple kraut for a few minutes, then finish by stirring in the crème fraîche. Season with salt and pepper.

For the caramelised apple, cut the apples into quarters, remove the cores and cut into thin wedges. Melt the butter in a frying pan over medium heat, then add the apple slices and sauté for 2–3 minutes. Add the sugar and caramelise, then deglaze the pan with the apple juice. Briefly boil the mixture, then season lightly with salt.

For the semolina dumplings, bring the milk to the boil in a small saucepan with the butter, salt and nutmeg. Rain the semolina into the pan and stir until well combined. Set aside to cool. Once cool, whisk in the eggs and set aside for 10 minutes. Using two teaspoons, form the semolina into small quenelles. Cook the dumplings in gently simmering salted water for 8–10 minutes.

Preheat the oven to 120°C (250°F) (conventional). Cut the char fillets in half. Grease a baking dish with the butter, then lay the fish in the dish, skin side down, and cover with the pancetta. Pick the thyme leaves and scatter over the fish, along with the capers. Season with salt and pepper and bake for 8–10 minutes, until the fish is transparent.

Spoon the apple kraut onto plates. Top with the caramelised apple, semolina dumplings and fish, and serve.

APPLE AND CELERY GAZPACHO
WITH LEMON OIL

In summer there's nothing more refreshing than a cold, light soup. The creaminess in this soup comes from the baguette, while the apple, lemon and celery take care of freshness and lightness. And last but not least, this recipe is a tasty way to use up stale bread.

Lemon oil
finely grated zest of 1 lemon
250 ml (8½ fl oz/1 cup) olive oil

Gazpacho
8–10 baguette slices
250 ml (8½ fl oz/1 cup) apple juice
60 ml (2 fl oz/¼ cup) apple cider vinegar

8–10 celery stalks (with leaves)
2–3 sour green or yellow apples
finely grated zest and juice of 1 lemon
250 ml (8½ fl oz/1 cup) vegetable stock or water
125 ml (4 fl oz/½ cup) orange juice
salt and freshly ground black pepper, to taste

For the lemon oil, mix the lemon zest with the olive oil and set aside to infuse.

Preheat the oven to 180°C (350°F) (conventional). For the gazpacho, soak five or six baguette slices in the apple juice and apple cider vinegar for a few minutes. Peel the celery and roughly chop, reserving the celery leaves for garnish. Core the apples and roughly chop, then purée the apple and celery in a blender with the remaining ingredients except the unsoaked bread slices. Refrigerate until ready to serve. Toast the remaining bread slices until golden brown.

Spoon the gazpacho into soup bowls. Garnish with a few drops of the lemon oil and the celery leaves. Crumble the toasted bread over the top and serve.

POTATO PANCAKES
WITH APPLE SAUCE

Potatoes with apples? When we were children this was something completely new, which we learned from the guests at Grandma's small guesthouse. We loved the combination and immediately named it potato pancakes. Then, during my time in California, I discovered that it's also a traditional Jewish recipe for Hanukkah, when potato latkes are eaten with sour cream and apple sauce.

Potato pancakes	1 egg	*Apple sauce*
4 large roasting potatoes	salt and freshly ground black pepper,	1 kg (2 lb 3 oz) apples
1 onion	to taste	200 ml (7 fl oz) apple juice or water
1 tablespoon plain (all-purpose)	freshly grated nutmeg, to taste	
flour	oil, for frying	

Peel and coarsely grate the potatoes. Dry immediately using a clean tea towel (dish towel), squeezing well to remove all excess moisture (you need to work quickly, to avoid the potato turning brown). Peel and grate the onion, and dry in the same way. Place in a bowl, along with the potato. Add the flour and egg, season with salt, pepper and nutmeg and stir well to combine.

Preheat the oven to 100°C (210°F) (conventional). Heat a little oil in a frying pan over medium heat and drop in tablespoons of the potato mixture. Press gently to flatten slightly and cook on both sides until golden brown. Drain on paper towel and keep warm in the oven.

For the apple sauce, peel, core and halve the apples, and cut into thick slices. Place the apple slices and apple juice or water in a large saucepan and simmer over medium heat for 20–30 minutes, until the apple falls apart. Gently mash the apple or purée in a blender if you prefer a very smooth sauce.

Serve the potato pancakes with the apple sauce.

ROAST PORK WITH APPLE CIDER, BAKED APPLES AND PURPLE POTATOES

The sweetness of the apples and the sourness of the apple cider give the pork belly a certain lightness. Pears or quinces also work well in this recipe.

1 carrot
1 small piece celeriac
8–10 small purple potatoes
8 French shallots
3–4 small apples
800 g (1 lb 12 oz) pork belly
1 tablespoon coarsely ground black pepper, plus extra to taste
1 teaspoon bread spices (available from specialist stores)
2 thyme sprigs
salt, to taste
150 ml (5 fl oz) apple cider

Preheat the oven to 190°C (375°F) (conventional). Peel the carrot and celeriac and cut into slices about 2 cm (¾ in) thick. Peel the potatoes and cut into quarters. Halve the shallots without peeling. Depending on their size, cut the apples into halves or quarters. Remove the cores.

Score the skin of the pork belly several times lengthways with a sharp knife. Season liberally with the pepper, bread spices and thyme, then place, skin side up, in a roasting tin. Add the carrot, celeriac, potato, shallot and apple, and season well with salt. Pour the apple cider around the meat and roast for 10–15, minutes until the pork skin is golden brown. Reduce the oven temperature to 150°C (300°F) and roast for a further 1½ hours, until cooked through and juicy. To finish, turn the grill (broiler) to maximum heat and grill the pork belly, skin side up, for about 10 minutes, to obtain a nice crackling.

Slice the pork belly and serve with the vegetables and apple.

PRESERVED APRICOTS

Apricots remind me of summer and the time I used to spend at my grandma's farm. It is one of my favourite childhood memories. My grandma was very fussy about the apricots she bought, as she'd make at least 100 jars of preserves each year. Sometimes we went with Grandpa to his vineyard in Lower Austria, where they grew their own apricot trees. When there was a glut, we entered a state of apricot frenzy – preserving, baking and freezing them like there was no tomorrow. And so even in winter, apricots could enhance raisin pancakes, semolina and quark dumplings, or semolina pudding.

1 vanilla bean
300 g (10½ oz) sugar
1 strip lemon zest
juice of ½ lemon
2–3 rosemary sprigs
1 kg (2 lb 3 oz) apricots

Split the vanilla bean lengthways. Place in a saucepan, along with the sugar, 1 litre (34 fl oz/4 cups) water, lemon zest and juice and rosemary. Bring to the boil.

Halve the apricots, remove the stones and pack them into sterilised preserving jars. Pour over the hot syrup, including the vanilla bean, rosemary and lemon zest, leaving 1 cm (½ in) free at the top of each jar. Seal tightly. Lay a clean tea towel (dish towel) in the base of a wide stockpot. Sit the jars in the pot and pour in enough hot water until it reaches just below the jar lids. Bring to the boil. Once air bubbles start to rise in the jars, reduce the heat and simmer for 10 minutes. Lift out the jars with tongs and allow to cool.

The preserved apricots will keep in a dark, cool place for about 1 year.

CHICKEN KORMA WITH
APRICOTS AND CASHEW NUTS

This korma is one of the tried-and-tested curry recipes from my time at Babette's in California, and it's still one of my favourites. The saffron isn't essential, but it does go well with the apricots. I like leaving some of the spices whole, so that later you bite into the wonderful whole seeds. A few drops of rosewater at the end makes this korma really special.

600 g (1 lb 5 oz) boneless chicken thighs
or 4–5 whole chicken thighs*
2–3 cm (¾–1¼ in) piece ginger
3 garlic cloves
200 g (7 oz) yoghurt, plus extra to serve
200 ml (7 fl oz) coconut milk
pinch of saffron threads
50 g (1¾ oz) cashew nuts, plus 1–2 tablespoons extra to finish
½ red chilli
60 g (2 oz) clarified butter
1 teaspoon poppy seeds
1 teaspoon fennel seeds
2 green cardamom pods, lightly bruised
1 teaspoon each black and yellow mustard seeds
1 teaspoon coriander seeds
1 teaspoon ground cumin
1 star anise
1 cinnamon stick
3 onions
300–400 ml (10–13½ fl oz) chicken or vegetable stock or water
½ teaspoon ground turmeric
pinch of sweet paprika
6 fresh or dried apricots
1 lime
1–2 drops rosewater (optional)
salt and freshly ground black pepper, to taste

* Boning the chicken thighs yourself allows you to make fresh chicken stock, which can be boiled very gently alongside the curry. Remove the cooked meat from the bone, then place the bones in a stockpot with your choice of root vegetables, 1 bay leaf, 1 slice of ginger and enough cold water to cover. Bring to the boil, then reduce the heat to very low and simmer for at least 30 minutes and up to 1½ hours. Regularly skim off any scum that rises to the surface and season lightly with salt at the end.

Cut the chicken into 3–4 cm (1¼–1½ in) pieces. Peel and finely chop the ginger and garlic and place in a large bowl. Add the yoghurt and chicken and mix well. Cover and marinate in the fridge for 12 hours. (Sometimes I only have a few hours available – and that's okay too.) Take the chicken out of the fridge 30 minutes before cooking, to come to room temperature. Gently warm the coconut milk in a small saucepan over low heat, then add the saffron threads and set aside to infuse. Soften the cashew nuts in 75–100 ml (2½–3½ fl oz) lukewarm water for about 20 minutes.

Cut the chilli in half lengthways, remove the seeds and finely chop. Heat half the clarified butter in a large frying pan, then fry the chilli and all the spices, from the poppy seeds to the cinnamon stick, until aromatic and the mustard seeds start to pop. Add the marinated chicken with the yoghurt and cook for 5–8 minutes. Transfer to a bowl and set aside.

Peel and halve the onions, finely dice and cook gently in the same frying pan in the remaining clarified butter, stirring frequently, for 8 minutes, or until soft and caramelised.

Purée the cashew nuts along with their soaking water, then add to the onion and cook, stirring, for 1–2 minutes. Return the chicken to the pan, along with the infused saffron coconut milk, stock or water, turmeric and paprika, then cover and cook over low heat for 30 minutes.

About 10 minutes before the end of cooking, halve the apricots, remove the stones and slice into wedges. If using dried apricots, slice them into thin strips and set a few aside for garnish. Wash the lime in very hot water, then finely grate the zest or peel off thin strips with a potato peeler. Squeeze the juice of the lime into the curry and add the apricot, zest and remaining cashew nuts. At the end of cooking, add the rosewater, if using, and season with salt and pepper. Finish with a drizzle of extra yoghurt.

Serve with steamed basmati rice, couscous or flatbreads.

If you feel like you're missing a vegetable accompaniment to this dish, you can simply add seasonal vegetables to the korma according to their cooking times, or blanch or sauté and serve alongside.

COLD APRICOT SOUP
WITH FENNEL

This soup is inspired by my visit to Bar Tartine in San Francisco, and I've tried to refine the recipe each year ever since that mild summer evening. The slice of bread makes the soup even creamier than it already is, but it can also be omitted. You can also add a hint of saffron or a star anise to balance this cold delicacy even further.

2 French shallots
1 fennel bulb
1 tablespoon olive oil
1 slice ginger
2 thyme sprigs
½ teaspoon fennel seeds
1 teaspoon salt, plus extra to taste
100 ml (3½ fl oz) vermouth
250 ml (8½ fl oz/1 cup) dry white wine
500 ml (17 fl oz/2 cups) vegetable stock
finely grated zest of 1 lemon

2 fresh or 4 dried bay leaves
1 kg (2 lb 3 oz) apricots
1–2 teaspoons honey, to taste (depending
on the sweetness of the apricots)
1 thick slice sourdough baguette or brioche
4 teaspoons white wine vinegar
freshly ground black pepper, to taste
150 g (5½ oz) cottage cheese, to garnish
shiso leaves, to garnish
almond oil, for drizzling

Halve and peel the shallots, then thinly slice. Remove the fronds from the fennel and set aside for garnish. Shave one-quarter of the fennel and also set aside for garnish. Slice the remaining fennel. Heat the olive oil in a large saucepan over low heat and sauté the shallot, sliced fennel, ginger and thyme sprigs for 5–8 minutes, until soft and transparent but not brown. Add the fennel seeds and salt. Deglaze the pan with the vermouth, then pour in the wine and stock. Add the lemon zest and bay leaves and simmer gently for at least 20 minutes.

Halve the apricots and remove the stones. Add the apricots (retaining a few for garnish) and honey to the pan, and simmer gently for a further 20 minutes. Remove from the heat, add the bread and vinegar, and allow to cool completely. Purée the soup, season with salt and pepper and chill in the fridge until ready to serve. Slice the reserved apricots into wedges. Spoon the soup into bowls, then top with the cottage cheese, shaved fennel, fennel fronds, shiso leaves and apricot wedges. Drizzle over a little almond oil, to finish.

APRICOT AND QUARK STRUDEL
WITH DANDELION ICE CREAM

Another classic to make during apricot season.
Whether in cakes or dumplings, apricots and soft cheese are simply perfect together!

Dandelion syrup
4 handfuls dandelion flowers
1 litre (34 fl oz/4 cups) lukewarm water
1 kg (2 lb 3 oz) caster (superfine) sugar
1 strip lemon zest
juice of 1 lemon

Dandelion ice cream
250 ml (8½ fl oz/1 cup) milk
100 ml (3½ fl oz) Dandelion syrup (see above)
2 tablespoons caster (superfine) sugar
6 egg yolks
scraped seeds of ½ vanilla bean
pinch of salt
500 ml (17 fl oz/2 cups) thickened (whipping) cream

Strudel pastry
200 g (7 oz) plain (all-purpose) flour,
plus extra for dusting
pinch of salt
2 tablespoons oil, plus extra for rubbing
110 ml (4 fl oz) lukewarm water

Filling
300 g (10½ oz) apricots
3 eggs
130 g (4½ oz) very soft butter
60 g (2 oz) caster (superfine) sugar
scraped seeds of ½ vanilla bean
500 g (1 lb 2 oz) quark
120 g (4½ oz) sour cream
½ teaspoon finely grated lemon zest
juice of 1 lemon
60 ml (2 fl oz/¼ cup) rum
1 tablespoon icing (confectioners') sugar, for dusting

For the dandelion syrup, combine the dandelion flowers and water in a large saucepan. Cover and leave for 3–4 hours to infuse. Bring the mixture to the boil, then leave overnight to infuse even further. Remove the flowers and stir the sugar and lemon zest into the liquid. Bring to the boil again, then add the lemon juice. Simmer over low heat until the syrup has the consistency of honey. Pour the hot syrup into sterilised jars. Well-sealed, the syrup will keep for up to 3 years.

For the dandelion ice cream, heat the milk, syrup, sugar, egg yolks, vanilla seeds and salt in a saucepan over low heat, stirring constantly, until the mixture gradually begins to thicken. Pour the cream into a large bowl, then add the warm milk mixture; this will immediately stop the cooking process. Stir the mixture to combine and refrigerate for 2–3 hours or overnight to infuse. Push the mixture through a sieve and churn in an ice-cream maker according to the manufacturer's instructions.

Preheat the oven to 180°C (350°F) (conventional). For the strudel pastry, combine the flour, salt, oil and water in a large bowl, then knead the mixture to a smooth, elastic dough. Form the dough into a ball and rub all over with a few extra drops of oil. Place the dough in a bowl, cover with a plate and leave at room temperature for 30 minutes.

For the filling, halve the apricots, remove the stones and cut into thick wedges. Separate the eggs and beat the egg whites to stiff peaks. Beat 60 g (2 oz) of the butter with the sugar and vanilla seeds until pale and fluffy. Gradually beat in the egg yolks, followed by the quark, sour cream, lemon zest and juice, and rum. Carefully fold in the beaten egg white.

Evenly dust a large tea towel (dish towel) with flour. Roll the dough out on the tea towel as thinly as possible. Place your hands under the pastry, palms down, and gently stretch the pastry thinner and thinner with the backs of your hands, working from the centre outwards. Keep going until you can see the tea towel underneath. Don't worry if the pastry tears a little; a few small holes are fine.

Melt the remaining butter and allow to cool. Brush the pastry with 3 tablespoons of the butter. Spread the filling over the pastry, leaving a 5 cm (2 in) border. Cover the quark mixture with the apricots. Fold in the pastry edges then, using the tea towel to assist you, gently roll up the strudel and slide, seam side down, onto a large baking sheet lined with baking paper. Brush with the remaining melted butter and bake for 35–40 minutes, until golden.

Dust the strudel with the icing sugar, then slice and serve with the ice cream.

APRICOT DUMPLINGS

My grandma often made 'topfennockerln' (quark dumplings) or 'marillenknödeln' (apricot dumplings) for us to enjoy after school. When I was eight years' old, my apricot dumpling record was nine pieces. Here's the original recipe.

Dumplings	*Crumb*
375 g (13 oz) quark	50 g (1¾ oz) breadcrumbs
30 g (1 oz) very soft butter	45 g (1½ oz) caster (superfine) sugar
3 egg yolks	½ teaspoon ground cinnamon
3 tablespoons milk	20 g (¾ oz) butter
50 g (1¾ oz/⅓ cup) plain (all-purpose) flour,	icing (confectioners') sugar, to serve
plus extra for dusting	
pinch of salt, plus ½ teaspoon extra	
8–10 apricots	
8–10 sugar cubes	
½ teaspoon caster (superfine) sugar	

For the dumplings, place the quark, butter, egg yolks and milk in a large bowl and mix until smooth. Add the flour and salt, then quickly form into a smooth dough. Refrigerate for 1 hour.

Carefully slice open the apricots without cutting all the way through. Remove the stones and replace with a sugar cube. Reclose the apricots. Fill a large saucepan with water, add the extra salt and the sugar, and bring to the boil.

On a lightly floured work surface, divide the dough into 8 evenly sized balls. Roll each ball into a flat disc, big enough to enclose one apricot. Place an apricot in the centre of the dough and wrap the dough around it, sealing well. Repeat with the remaining dough and apricots, making sure the dumplings are as round as possible. Slide the dumplings into the boiling water, then reduce the heat to very low and cook, covered, for 15–20 minutes.

For the crumb, toast the breadcrumbs, sugar, cinnamon and butter in a frying pan until golden. Lift the dumplings out of the water, drain briefly on paper towel and roll in the crumb mixture. Serve the dumplings on a plate with the remaining crumbs and a dusting of icing sugar.

SARDINES STUFFED WITH
COUSCOUS AND APRICOTS

This was one of the many dishes we enjoyed during a farmstay in Sicily. Sicilian antipasti is generous in size and complexity, with some entrées alone comprising six to eight components. I guarantee there won't be any leftovers after making this dish.

Stuffing
150 g (5½ oz) couscous
½ teaspoon ras el hanout
1 teaspoon salt, plus extra to taste
60 ml (2 fl oz/¼ cup) olive oil
juice of 1 orange
3–4 apricots
4–6 black or green olives
30 g (1 oz) pine nuts
1 small bunch parsley
1 small bunch mint
½ teaspoon finely grated lemon zest
juice of 1 lemon
freshly ground black pepper, to taste

Sardines
1 teaspoon butter
1 fennel bulb
2 tablespoons olive oil
juice of 1 orange
12 butterflied sardine fillets
1 garlic clove
3–4 fresh or 4–5 dried bay leaves
4 teaspoons white wine
salt and freshly ground black pepper,
for seasoning

For the stuffing, place the couscous, ras el hanout, salt, half the olive oil and the orange juice in a bowl. Pour in enough boiling water to cover the couscous by about 1 cm (½ in) and stir well once. Cover, and leave for 10 minutes to swell. Carefully fluff up the couscous with a fork. Halve the apricots, remove the stones and cut into small dice. Pit the olives and finely chop. Toast the pine nuts in a dry frying pan, and finely chop the parsley and mint leaves. Add the apricot, olives, pine nuts and herbs to the couscous, along with the lemon zest and juice and remaining olive oil. Fluff everything together with a fork, then season with salt and pepper. Set aside for 30 minutes for the flavours to infuse.

For the sardines, preheat the oven to 180°C (350°F) (conventional). Grease an ovenproof dish with the butter. Thinly slice the fennel and spread it over the bottom of the dish. Drizzle over half the olive oil and the orange juice, and season with salt and pepper.

Wash the sardines and pat dry with paper towel. Lay the sardines flat, skin side down, and add about 1 tablespoon of the couscous mixture to each fish. Roll up tightly and place, seam side down, in the prepared dish. Lightly bruise the garlic clove and place in the dish along with the bay leaves. Drizzle the wine and remaining olive oil over the sardines and bake for 15–20 minutes.

APRICOT CLOUD CAKE
WITH ROSE CREAM

Cake and ice cream in one bite – it's not only children whose hearts beat faster!

Cloud cake
100 g (3½ oz) butter
180 g (6½ oz) egg whites
(about 5–6)
250 g (9 oz) caster (superfine) sugar
160 g (5½ oz) plain (all-purpose) flour
1 heaped tablespoon potato starch
1 teaspoon baking powder

Apricot iced parfait
8 large ripe apricots
juice of ½ lemon
150 g (5½ oz) caster (superfine) sugar
5 egg yolks
200 ml (7 fl oz) milk
300 ml (10 fl oz) thickened (whipping)
cream
pinch of salt

Rose cream
1 cardamom pod
2 teaspoons icing (confectioners') sugar
scraped seeds of ½ vanilla bean
250 ml (8½ fl oz/1 cup) thickened
(whipping) cream
a few drops rosewater
rose petals and apricots, to garnish
(optional)

Preheat the oven to 180°C (350°F) (conventional). Line a baking tray with baking paper. For the cake, melt the butter and allow to cool. Beat the egg whites and 2 tablespoons of the sugar to stiff peaks. Sift the remaining ingredients into the beaten egg white and carefully fold in. To finish, fold in the melted butter. Spread the cake mixture over the prepared tray until it is about 2 cm (¾ in) thick and bake for 18–20 minutes until golden.

For the parfait, remove the stones from six of the apricots and roughly chop. Combine the apricots, lemon juice and 50 g (1¾ oz) of the sugar in a large bowl and set aside for 20 minutes, then purée until smooth. Remove the stones from the remaining apricots and cut into small pieces.

Beat the egg yolks with the remaining sugar until creamy. Bring the milk to the boil in a saucepan and pour into the egg yolk mixture, stirring constantly. Return the whole lot to the saucepan and stir over low heat until creamy. Remove from the heat and beat over a bowl filled with ice cubes until cool, or cool in the fridge. Beat the cream with

the salt, then fold into the egg and milk mixture in two batches. Stir the apricot purée into the parfait mixture, then divide the mixture in half and add the apricot pieces to one half.

Line a loaf (bar) tin with baking paper (this works best if you grease it first with softened butter). Spread the apricot parfait with the added apricot pieces in the tin and freeze for 2 hours. Refrigerate the remaining parfait mixture. Cut the cake into two pieces to fit the tin and lay one piece on top of the frozen parfait layer. Now spread the remaining apricot parfait over the top, add the remaining layer of cake and freeze for at least 2 hours.

For the rose cream, remove the cardamom seeds from the pod and, using a mortar and pestle, crush the seeds with the icing sugar and vanilla seeds. Beat the cream with the spiced sugar and rosewater until thick but not too firm. Remove the cake from the fridge 10–15 minutes before serving, then turn out of the tin and slice. Serve with the rose cream and, if you like, garnish with rose petals and extra apricots.

B

BLACKBERRIES, BLUEBERRIES

TAGLIATELLE WITH PORCINI MUSHROOMS AND BLACKBERRIES

This dish is a classic among my recipes. The combination originated after I was out looking for porcini mushrooms and found blackberries at the same time. These two woodland companions get along so well together!

Pasta dough
300 g (10½ oz) '00' flour, plus extra for dusting
3 whole eggs or 5 egg yolks
1 tablespoon water

Porcini and blackberries
200 g (7 oz) fresh porcini mushrooms
3 tablespoons olive oil, plus extra to serve
2 thyme sprigs
salt, to taste
2 small red onions

1 garlic clove
½ teaspoon bread spices (available from specialist stores)
200 g (7 oz) blackberries
freshly ground black pepper, to taste
grated parmesan, to serve

For the pasta dough, heap the flour onto a clean work surface, make a well in the middle and add the eggs or egg yolks and water. Gently whisk the eggs and water with a fork then, little by little, mix in the flour from the edges until you have a rough dough. Knead with your hands for 8–10 minutes, until the dough is smooth and elastic. Wrap in plastic wrap and refrigerate for about 20 minutes.

Roll the dough out as thinly as possible, either on a floured work surface using a rolling pin or with a pasta machine. Dust both sides of the dough well with flour, then roll the dough up loosely and slice into tagliatelle strips. Leave the tagliatelle to dry a little on a baking sheet dusted with flour, loosening the strips up now and then to ensure they don't stick together.

Clean the mushrooms and cut in half or slice them depending on their size. Heat 1 tablespoon of the olive oil in a frying pan and add the mushrooms and thyme. Cook, stirring frequently, until the mushrooms are browned, then season lightly with salt. Remove from the pan and set aside. Peel and thinly slice the onions and garlic. Heat the remaining olive oil, then fry the onion and garlic for 3–5 minutes, stirring. Add the bread spices and mushrooms, along with any residual liquid. To finish, stir in the blackberries and season with salt and pepper.

Cook the tagliatelle for less than 1 minute in simmering salted water, then drain, reserving a few spoonfuls of the cooking water. Return the tagliatelle to the pan and add the cooking water and mushroom and berry mixture. Stir well to combine, drizzle with extra olive oil and serve with parmesan.

DUCK BREAST WITH BLACKBERRIES
AND SILVERBEET

Duck really lends itself to sweet accompaniments! If blackberries aren't available, you can substitute cherries or blueberries. Purple potatoes baked in the reserved duck fat go particularly well with this dish.

4 duck breasts (about 150 g/5½ oz each)
salt and freshly ground black pepper
1 teaspoon garam masala or mixed spice
4–6 small French shallots
250 g (9 oz) silverbeet (Swiss chard)
1 sage sprig

1 tablespoon honey
125 ml (4 fl oz/½ cup) red wine
100 ml (3½ fl oz) duck or chicken stock
150 g (5½ oz) blackberries
1 tablespoon cold butter

Preheat the oven to 120°C (250°F) (conventional). Score the skin on the duck breasts with a sharp knife in a lattice pattern, taking care not to cut into the meat itself. Season both sides with salt, pepper and garam masala. Heat a cast-iron frying pan over high heat and gently place the duck breasts, skin side down, in the pan. Cook for 3–5 minutes, then turn over and cook for a further 1–2 minutes. Transfer the duck, skin side down, to an ovenproof dish and bake for 10–15 minutes.

Remove all but 2 tablespoons of the duck fat from the frying pan and set aside. Peel and halve the shallots, then add to the frying pan and cook until golden brown. Cut the silverbeet stems into 3–5 cm (1¼–2 in) lengths and set the leaves aside. Pick the sage leaves and add to the pan with the silverbeet stalks and fry until softened. Caramelise the mixture with the honey, then deglaze the pan with the wine and pour in the stock. Reduce the liquid by about one-third, then stir in the blackberries and cold butter. Season with salt and pepper. Add the silverbeet leaves and cook in the sauce for 2–3 minutes, until wilted.

Remove the duck breasts from the oven and cut into slices. Divide the silverbeet and blackberry mixture among plates and arrange the duck breast on top.

BLACKBERRY COBBLER

There could hardly be an easier dessert. If you don't have any ground almonds, try using other nuts; they will taste just as good and can add crunch to the dough when more roughly chopped. Rolled (porridge) oats, muesli, seeds, spices or pieces of chocolate also work well in the dough.

400 g (14 oz) blackberries
100 g (3½ oz) caster (superfine) sugar
1 tablespoon cornflour (cornstarch)
1 tablespoon lemon juice
100 g (3½ oz) plain (all-purpose) flour
60 g (2 oz) ground almonds
pinch of salt
1 teaspoon baking powder
2 cardamom pods
½ teaspoon finely grated lemon zest
100 g (3½ oz) cold butter
1 egg
vanilla ice cream (page 186), to serve

Preheat the oven to 180°C (350°F) (conventional). In a bowl, mix the blackberries with half the sugar, the cornflour and lemon juice. Spread the mixture out in an ovenproof dish.

In the same bowl, combine the flour, ground almonds, salt, baking powder and remaining sugar. Break open the cardamom pods and crush the seeds using a mortar and pestle. Add the crushed seeds and the lemon zest to the bowl. Using your fingers, rub the butter into the dry ingredients until the mixture resembles breadcrumbs, then add the egg and mix to form a dough. Cover the berries with dollops of the dough and bake for 25–30 minutes, until the cobbler is golden brown.

Serve with vanilla ice cream.

BLACKBERRY
SORBET

With its sweet and sour fruitiness, this sorbet refreshes the palate – and the head – as a dessert or palate cleanser between courses.

---

100 g (3½ oz) caster (superfine) sugar
juice of ½ lemon
500 g (1 lb 2 oz) blackberries, plus extra to garnish

In a small saucepan, bring the sugar and 100 ml (3½ fl oz) water to the boil and simmer over low heat for 5–10 minutes, until you have a syrup. Allow the syrup to cool a little, then transfer to a blender, along with the lemon juice and blackberries. Purée the mixture, then transfer to an airtight container and freeze overnight.

Remove the sorbet from the freezer 30 minutes before serving. If you like, pop the extra blackberries in the freezer to firm up a little.

Serve the sorbet in bowls or on individual spoons, garnished with blackberries.

BRAISED DIJON RABBIT
WITH BLUEBERRIES

Already a true classic in my kitchen, and just as good with chicken!
If you don't have blueberries, elderberries or blackberries also taste great with this.

4 small rabbit legs
salt and freshly ground black pepper
4 French shallots
2 garlic cloves
olive oil, for frying
3 strips lemon zest
4 fresh bay leaves
200 ml (7 fl oz) dry white wine

400 ml (13½ fl oz) chicken stock
½ bunch chervil
½ bunch tarragon
200 g (7 oz) crème fraîche
1 tablespoon wholegrain mustard
1 tablespoon dijon mustard
½ teaspoon ground turmeric
2 teaspoons cornflour (cornstarch)

4 celery stalks
100 g (3½ oz) green olives
50 g (1¾ oz) capers, rinsed and
squeezed dry
100 g (3½ oz) blueberries
3–4 tablespoons grape juice or water
creamy polenta, to serve

Preheat the oven to 150°C (300°F) (conventional). Season the rabbit legs with salt and pepper. Peel and thinly slice the shallots, then peel and finely chop the garlic. Heat a little olive oil in a flameproof casserole dish on the stovetop and brown the rabbit well on both sides for 2–3 minutes. Remove the rabbit and set aside. Add the shallot to the dish and sauté for 5–8 minutes, stirring frequently. Add the garlic, lemon zest and bay leaves and fry for 1 minute, then deglaze the pan with the wine.

Place the rabbit legs back in the dish and pour over the stock. Cover with foil, then transfer to the oven and cook for 2–2½ hours, until the meat starts to fall off the bones. Remove the dish from the oven and carefully lift the rabbit legs out of the sauce. Chop the herbs and stir into the sauce, along with the crème fraîche, both mustards, turmeric and cornflour. Whisk to combine. Peel the celery and thickly slice on the diagonal, then add to the sauce, along with the olives and capers.

Return the rabbit legs to the dish, then cook for a further 5–10 minutes on the stovetop. Season with salt and pepper.

Combine the blueberries and the grape juice or water in a small saucepan and simmer for a few minutes.

Spoon the polenta onto serving plates and top with the rabbit legs and sauce. Finish with the blueberries and a drizzle of grape juice.

BLUEBERRY PANCAKES

As kids, we often spent our summers on my grandma's farm in local alpine pastures. One of my fondest memories was the mountains of small blueberry cakes, slices, dumplings and pancakes. To make them, first we had to gather the dark-blue berries, resulting in not only our hands, but also our lips and tongues turning blue.

This dish is wonderful to make if you are on holiday, because you only need a cup and a tablespoon to measure out the ingredients!

310 g (11 oz / 2 cups) blueberries
1 tablespoon caster (superfine) sugar
125 ml (4 fl oz / ½ cup) milk or water
150 g (5½ oz / 1 cup) plain (all-purpose) flour
1 tablespoon clarified butter
icing (confectioners') sugar, to serve

In a bowl, mix the blueberries, caster sugar and milk or water. Stir in the flour until completely combined. Melt the clarified butter in a frying pan and fry tablespoons of the blueberry mixture for 2–3 minutes on both sides. Serve dusted with icing sugar.

EASY POTATO FLOUR
KUGELHOPF

A 'kugelhopf' could hardly be easier.
This recipe was handed down from 'Aunty Hedi'.
At least that's what it says in Grandma's handwritten recipe book.
Thanks, Aunty Hedi!

butter, for greasing
flour, for dusting
6 eggs
50 g (1¾ oz) caster (superfine) sugar
150 g (5½ oz) icing (confectioners') sugar
juice of 1 lemon
1 teaspoon finely grated lemon zest
130 g (4½ oz) potato flour
1 teaspoon baking powder
250 g (9 oz) blueberries, plus a few extra for decoration

Grease a kugelhopf tin with butter and dust with flour. Refrigerate until ready to use. Preheat the oven to 180°C (350°F) (conventional).

Separate the eggs. Beat the egg whites with the caster sugar to firm peaks. Sift 100 g (3½ oz) of the icing sugar into a bowl and beat in the egg yolks until foaming and creamy. Stir half the lemon juice and the lemon zest into the egg yolk mixture. Sift the potato flour and baking powder into a small bowl. Alternating with the beaten egg whites, fold the potato flour mixture into the egg yolk mixture until well combined. Finally, fold in the blueberries. Spoon the mixture into the kugelhopf tin, then transfer to the middle shelf of the oven and bake for 1 hour. Allow to cool a little, then turn out of the tin.

Mix the remaining icing sugar with as much of the remaining lemon juice as necessary to make a smooth icing (frosting). Drizzle the icing over the cake and decorate with the extra blueberries.

BLUEBERRY LIQUEUR

I still have a big ceramic pot with its cork stopper that used to be filled with blueberry liqueur. It would sit on various windowsills, until the liqueur was fully mature.

800 g–1 kg (1 lb 12 oz–2 lb 3 oz) blueberries
500 ml (17 fl oz/2 cups) vodka or any neutral-grain spirit
500 g (1 lb 2 oz) sugar
1 vanilla bean
1 strip lemon zest
1 cinnamon stick

Tip the blueberries into a large, sterilised sealable jar or a rumtopf (rum pot) and pour over the vodka.

Boil the sugar and 500 ml (17 fl oz/2 cups) water for 5–8 minutes, until you have a syrup. Split the vanilla bean lengthways, scrape out the seeds and add them to the syrup, along with the vanilla bean, lemon zest and cinnamon stick.

Pour the spiced syrup over the blueberries and seal the jar well. Leave in a sunny spot for 6–8 weeks to mature. Shake regularly, so that the alcohol mixes with the blueberries.

Strain the blueberry liqueur, then pour into sterilised bottles with an airtight seal.

The liqueur will keep in a cool, dark place for a few years.

ZANDER TARTARE WITH BLUEBERRIES, CONFIT EGG YOLK AND CRISPBREAD

A recipe for which I have to thank my first holiday in Sweden. Instead of halibut, I've used zander here, but Arctic char or trout also work well – and then the marinating time can even be shortened a little. It's best to bake the crispbread the day before, so there's room in the oven for the eggs.

Crispbread
100 g (3½ oz) rye flour
100 g (3½ oz) rolled (porridge) oats
150 g (5½ oz) oat bran
50 g (1¾ oz) sesame seeds
60 g (2 oz) linseeds (flax seeds)
120 g (4½ oz) mixed nuts and seeds
(e.g. pepitas/pumpkin seeds, slivered almonds, sunflower seeds)
2 teaspoons salt

2 teaspoons bread spices (available from specialist stores)

Confit egg yolks
300–400 ml (10–13½ fl oz) olive oil
4 eggs

Zander tartare
200 g (7 oz) blueberries, plus extra to garnish

juice of 1 lemon
500 g (1 lb 2 oz) skinless, boneless zander, Arctic char or trout fillets
1 teaspoon lime juice
salt and freshly ground black pepper

To serve
watercress
olive oil

Preheat the oven to 190°C (375°F) (conventional). Line two baking sheets with baking paper. For the crispbread, combine all of the ingredients and 700 ml (23½ fl oz) water in a bowl and leave for 30 minutes for the grains to swell. Spread the mixture on the prepared baking sheets until it is very thin and smooth. Bake on the middle shelf of the oven for about 45 minutes, until the bread is lovely and crisp.

For the confit egg yolks, reduce the oven temperature to 65°C (150°F) (conventional). Pour the oil into an ovenproof dish and warm in the oven. Separate the eggs and very carefully lay the yolks in the warm olive oil. Cook in the oven for 35 minutes.

For the zander tartare, place the blueberries and lemon juice in a small saucepan and bring to the boil. Cook, stirring frequently, until the blueberries start to stew. Pass the mixture through a sieve, retaining the juice. Discard the pulp. Dice the fish, then place in a bowl, along with the blueberry juice and lime juice. Season with salt and pepper and refrigerate for 10–15 minutes to marinate.

Serve the tartare with the crispbread, confit egg yolks, extra blueberries and a little watercress. Finish with a drizzle of olive oil.

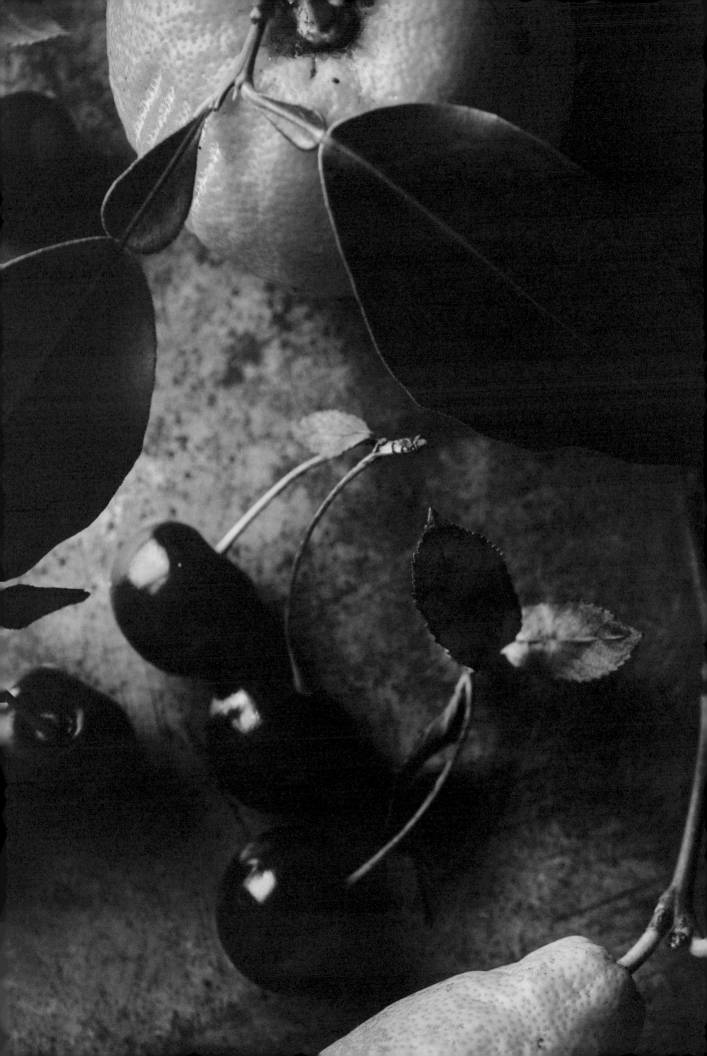

C

CHERRIES, CITRUS FRUITS, CURRANTS

CONFIT GUINEA FOWL LEGS WITH BALSAMIC CHERRIES ON CAULIFLOWER MASH

The fine art of confiting is an excellent preparation and preservation technique.
The meat only needs a few minutes in the oven before serving.

Confit guinea fowl legs
1 French shallot
1 garlic bulb
4 parsley sprigs
2 thyme sprigs
4 guinea fowl legs
2 tablespoons salt
1 teaspoon coarsely ground
black pepper
800 g (1 lb 12 oz) duck fat
or clarified butter

2 cloves
1 bay leaf
2 celery stalks
3–4 carrots

Cauliflower mash
1 cauliflower
200 ml (7 fl oz) milk
100 ml (3½ fl oz) chicken
or vegetable stock
1 tablespoon butter
1 teaspoon salt

Balsamic cherries
200 g (7 oz) cherries
4–6 French shallots
1 tablespoon butter
3 thyme sprigs
2 juniper berries
1 cinnamon stick
60 ml (2 fl oz/¼ cup) port
60 ml (2 fl oz/¼ cup)
balsamic vinegar

For the guinea fowl, peel and very finely chop the shallot and half the garlic cloves. Chop the parsley and pick the thyme leaves. Wash the guinea fowl legs and pat dry with paper towel. Transfer to a large bowl, then rub with the salt, pepper, shallot, garlic, parsley and thyme. Cover, and marinate in the fridge for 18–24 hours. Wash the marinade off the meat and pat dry.

Melt the duck fat in a stockpot. Add the guinea fowl legs, the remaining garlic cloves, the cloves, bay leaf, celery stalks and carrots, and cook over low heat for 2 hours. Remove from the heat and set aside.

For the cauliflower mash, roughly chop the cauliflower head and stalk. Place in a large saucepan, along with the milk, stock, butter and salt, and cook over low heat for 15–20 minutes, until soft. Purée and season to taste.

Preheat the oven to 200°C (400°F) (conventional). Remove the guinea fowl legs from the fat, scraping away any excess. Lay the legs in a roasting tin and roast for 15–20 minutes, until the skin is brown and crisp.

For the balsamic cherries, cut the cherries in half and remove the stones. Peel and halve the shallots, then cut into wedges. Sauté the shallot in the butter, along with the thyme, juniper berries and cinnamon stick until soft, then add the port and vinegar. Add the cherries and cook for 5–10 minutes, until you have a syrupy sauce.

Serve the guinea fowl legs on a bed of cauliflower mash and top with the balsamic cherries.

LENTIL AND WILD RICE SALAD WITH CHERRIES, RED SORREL AND SOFT GOAT'S CHEESE

This fresh summer salad is filling and a great addition to any barbecue.
Instead of goat's cheese, pieces of smoked fish also work well.

4 small beetroot (beets)
salt
100 g (3½ oz) beluga lentils
100 g (3½ oz) wild rice
1 French shallot
1 tablespoon butter
1 garlic clove
1 bay leaf
1–2 thyme sprigs

3–4 tarragon sprigs
200 g (7 oz) cherries
50 g (1¾ oz) hazelnuts
50 g (1¾ oz) peppery salad leaves (e.g.
red sorrel, young beetroot/beet leaves,
rocket/arugula or baby spinach)
1 handful fresh mixed herbs
150 g (5½ oz) soft goat's cheese in ash

Dressing
100 ml (3½ fl oz) olive oil
juice of 1 orange
1 teaspoon dijon mustard
juice of ½ lemon
2–3 tablespoons red wine vinegar
1 teaspoon honey

Preheat the oven to 200°C (400°F) (conventional). Trim the beetroot and place in an ovenproof dish. Fill the dish 2 cm (¾ in) deep with water, season with salt and cover tightly with foil. Roast for 40–50 minutes (depending on their size), until soft. Allow to cool a little, then peel. Cut the beetroot into thin wedges.

Wash the lentils and rice. Peel and finely dice the shallot. Melt the butter in a saucepan and sauté the shallot for a few minutes until translucent. Peel and finely chop the garlic, then add to the pan, along with the bay leaf, thyme, lentils and rice. Pour in enough water to cover the mixture by 2 cm (¾ in) and stir in 1 teaspoon of salt. Bring to the boil, then reduce the heat to low and simmer for 30–35 minutes. Set aside to cool. Remove the bay leaf and thyme sprigs.

Meanwhile, pick the tarragon leaves and tear the larger leaves into smaller pieces. Halve the cherries and remove the stones. Toast the hazelnuts in a dry frying pan, then peel, roughly chop and allow to cool.

For the dressing, combine all the ingredients in a screw-top jar, seal tightly and shake well.

In a salad bowl, carefully toss the lentil and wild rice mixture with the tarragon, cherries, hazelnuts, beetroot, salad leaves, herbs and two-thirds of the dressing. Divide the salad among plates, crumble over the goat's cheese and drizzle with the remaining dressing.

CHERRY
CLAFOUTIS

Traditional, simple and good. At the peak of the fruit season, there's nothing more quick and simple than this sweet pudding. For the cherry stones to impart their almond-like flavour, the stones should not, or rather must not, be removed from the cherries. Just remember to point this out to your guests before serving!

butter, for greasing
120 g (4½ oz) caster (superfine) sugar, plus extra for sprinkling
500 ml (17 fl oz/2 cups) milk
scraped seeds of ½ vanilla bean
pinch of salt
3 eggs
50 g (1¾ oz) plain (all-purpose) flour
1 teaspoon cherry schnapps or orange-flavoured liqueur
250–300 g (9–10½ oz) cherries
50 g (1¾ oz) icing (confectioners') sugar

Preheat the oven to 180°C (350°F) (conventional). Grease an ovenproof dish with butter and sprinkle with the extra sugar.

Combine the milk, sugar, vanilla seeds and salt in a small saucepan and warm over low heat until the sugar is dissolved but the mixture is not yet boiling. Mix one of the eggs with the flour in a bowl until smooth. Add the remaining eggs and mix again until smooth. Stirring constantly, slowly add the egg and flour mixture to the hot milk. Add the cherry schnapps or orange liqueur, then pour the batter into the prepared dish. Press the cherries into the batter.

Bake the clafoutis for 30–35 minutes until golden brown, then remove from the oven and sprinkle with the icing sugar. Switch the oven to the grill (broiler) and heat to 250°C (480°F). Return the clafoutis to the highest shelf and caramelise the top for 5–8 minutes. Allow to cool slightly; it is best enjoyed warm.

CHERRY TIRAMISU

Whether in tiramisu, trifle or parfait, mascarpone, coffee and chocolate are best friends, always good eaten with cherries.

450 g (1 lb) cherries
3 eggs
pinch of salt
100 g (3½ oz) icing (confectioners') sugar
250 g (9 oz) mascarpone
250 g (9 oz) ricotta
pinch of finely grated orange zest
scraped seeds of ½ vanilla bean
200 ml (7 fl oz) cooled strong espresso coffee
2 tablespoons amaretto or rum
200–300 g (7–10½ oz) savoiardi (lady fingers)
1 tablespoon unsweetened (Dutch) cocoa powder and/or
roughly chopped chocolate

Halve the cherries and remove the stones. Separate the eggs. Beat the egg whites and salt to stiff peaks. Beat the egg yolks with the icing sugar for 5 minutes, until creamy and almost white. In a large bowl, mix the mascarpone, ricotta, orange zest and vanilla seeds until smooth, then fold into the egg yolk mixture. Carefully fold in the beaten egg white.

In a shallow bowl, combine the espresso with the amaretto or rum. Briefly soak the savoiardi one at a time in the coffee mixture and use to line the bottom of an ovenproof dish. Spread over a layer of the egg mixture, then a layer of cherries. Add another layer of savoiardi, egg mixture and cherries, then finish with a final layer of egg mixture. Refrigerate for at least 3 hours, but preferably overnight. Just before serving, dust with the cocoa powder and/or chopped chocolate.

NETTLE AND CHERRY PIZZA

Nettle pizza is another recipe from the famous Chez Panisse family.

Dough
500 g (1 lb 2 oz) '00' flour, plus extra
for dusting
21 g (¾ oz) fresh yeast
1 teaspoon sugar
300 ml (10 fl oz) lukewarm water
1 teaspoon salt
1 tablespoon olive oil

Basil pesto
20 g (¾ oz) parmesan
1 handful pine nuts
1 bunch basil
½ teaspoon finely grated
lemon zest
juice of ½ lemon
250 ml (8½ fl oz/1 cup) olive oil
salt and freshly ground black pepper,
to taste

Topping
20 g (¾ oz) parmesan or pecorino
250 g (9 oz) ricotta
2–3 tablespoons olive oil
125 g (4½ oz) ball buffalo mozzarella
2–3 tablespoons basil pesto
5–6 stinging nettle stalks
100 g (3½ oz) cherries

For the dough, mix 2 tablespoons of the flour with the yeast, sugar and 50 ml (1¾ fl oz) of the water in a bowl. Cover with a tea towel (dish towel) and leave for 10–15 minutes in a warm place, until small bubbles appear at the surface. Combine the remaining flour and the salt in a large bowl and make a well in the centre. Pour the yeast mixture into the well, along with the remaining water and the olive oil, and combine to make a rough dough. Knead the dough on a well-floured work surface for 5 minutes into a supple, smooth dough. Cover and leave for 1 hour.

Knead the dough again on a lightly floured work surface, then divide into four evenly sized balls. Cover the dough balls and set aside for a further 25 minutes.

Place a pizza stone or an upside-down baking tray on the top shelf of the oven and heat to 250°C (480°F) (conventional).

For the pesto, finely grate the parmesan. Toast the pine nuts in a dry frying pan. Purée all the ingredients in a blender and season with salt and pepper.

For the topping, finely grate the parmesan or pecorino and mix with the ricotta, 1 tablespoon of the olive oil and salt and pepper to taste. On a lightly floured work surface, roll the dough balls into thin discs. Spread the topping evenly over the pizza bases. Tear over the mozzarella and drizzle over the pesto. Carefully pull the nettle leaves off the stems (it is best to wear gloves) and scatter over the pizza. Drizzle over the remaining olive oil and sprinkle over a little extra salt. Bake the pizzas, one at a time, for 12–18 minutes, until the edge of the base is brown and crisp.

Halve the cherries, remove the stones and scatter over the pizzas just before serving.

BLOOD ORANGE SALAD
WITH BEETROOT AND AVOCADO

A textbook Californian entrée salad.
It's also excellent with crumbled goat's cheese or burrata.

1 each of small yellow, red and
target beetroot (beets)
salt, to taste
3–4 blood oranges
1 small fennel bulb
1 avocado
2–3 mint sprigs
freshly ground black pepper, to taste

Dressing
1 teaspoon dijon mustard
60 ml (2 fl oz/¼ cup) olive oil
1 tablespoon elderflower vinegar
(page 98)
juice of ½ lemon
juice of ½ blood orange

Preheat the oven to 200°C (400°F) (conventional). Place the beetroot
in an ovenproof dish and pour in water to a depth of 2 cm (¾ in).
Season with salt and seal well with foil. Bake for 40–50 minutes
(depending on their size), until soft. Allow to cool a little, then peel
with your hands and cut into wedges. Peel the blood oranges and
remove the white pith. Thinly slice the oranges and arrange on four
plates, along with the beetroot.

For the dressing, combine all the ingredients in a screw-top jar, seal
tightly and shake well.

Shave the fennel and marinate in a little of the dressing. Halve the
avocado and remove the stone, then spoon out and slice the flesh. Pick
the mint leaves. Arrange all the ingredients on the orange slices and
beetroot in a decorative way, drizzle over the dressing and season with
salt and pepper.

CEVICHE WITH GRAPEFRUIT
AND LIME

*Curing fish with acid is traditional in southern European countries,
and there's nothing faster, simpler or better.*

400 g (14 oz) extremely fresh skinless Arctic char or trout fillets
juice of 3 limes
1 cm (½ in) piece ginger
½ teaspoon sesame seeds
½ teaspoon sesame oil
1 teaspoon olive oil
fleur de sel, to taste
4 radishes
1 grapefruit
freshly ground black pepper, to taste
1 punnet micro purple watercress

Wash the fish fillets under cold water, then pat dry with paper towel.
Pinbone if necessary. Thinly slice the fish and place in a non-reactive
bowl. Set aside 1 teaspoon of the lime juice, then pour the rest over the
fish. Cover with plastic wrap and refrigerate for at least 20 minutes.

Finely grate the ginger and mix with the sesame seeds, sesame oil, olive
oil and reserved lime juice in a small bowl to make a marinade. Divide
the fish among plates, then season with fleur de sel and the marinade.

Finely shave the radishes and spread over the ceviche. Peel the grapefruit
and remove the white pith. Slice the grapefruit or cut the segments from
the membranes and scatter over the ceviche. Season with pepper and
garnish with the watercress.

LEMON
POUND CAKE

Pound cake is an American classic. It's often served with a sugar glaze or cream-cheese icing (frosting), although I like it best with thick Greek-style yoghurt or home-made crème fraîche*.

380 g (13½ oz) plain (all-purpose) flour, plus extra for dusting
1 teaspoon baking powder
pinch of salt
finely grated zest of 3–4 lemons
300 g (10½ oz) caster (superfine) sugar
250 g (9 oz) butter, softened, plus extra for greasing
3 eggs
250 ml (8½ fl oz/1 cup) buttermilk
2 tablespoons lemon juice

Preheat the oven to 170°C (340°F) (conventional). Grease a 24 cm (9½ in) fluted bundt tin with the extra butter and dust with the extra flour. Combine the flour, baking powder and salt in a large bowl. In a second bowl, use your fingertips to thoroughly rub the lemon zest into the sugar. Beat the butter and lemon sugar in a stand mixer until creamy. Beat in the eggs one at time. With the mixer on its lowest setting, fold in the buttermilk and the flour mixture in batches, alternating between the two. Finally, fold in the lemon juice.

Pour the mixture into the prepared tin and bake on the middle shelf of the oven for 50 minutes, or until a skewer inserted into the cake comes out clean. Allow to cool, then remove from the tin.

*   It's really easy to make your own crème fraîche using left-over buttermilk. Mix 50 ml (1¾ fl oz) buttermilk with 250 ml (8½ fl oz/1 cup) thickened (whipping) cream, cover and leave at room temperature for 12–18 hours, then mature for 3–4 days in the fridge. Stir regularly throughout. It will keep for 2–3 weeks.

CITRUS SORBET

*Mixed with prosecco, this becomes
the Italian classic: 'sgroppino'.*

160 g (5½ oz) caster (superfine) sugar
250 ml (8½ fl oz/1 cup) freshly squeezed citrus juice
(e.g. lemon, orange, grapefruit or a mix)
juice of ½ lemon
2 teaspoons orange-flavoured liqueur

In a saucepan over medium heat, boil the sugar and
225 ml (7½ fl oz) water until the sugar dissolves. Remove
from the heat and allow to cool.

Pass the citrus and lemon juice through a fine-meshed
sieve, then stir into the sugar syrup, along with the
liqueur. Pour the citrus syrup into an ice-cream maker
and churn, according to the manufacturer's instructions,
for about 20 minutes, or until creamy. Alternatively,
freeze for 12 hours, stirring now and then with a fork.

ORANGE AND ALMOND CAKE

A recipe for which I have the lovely Jill Halek to thank and one that I've constantly built into my menus for ten years now, always to great applause. The cake tastes just as good made with three mandarins instead of the orange and lemon.

1 orange
1 lemon
butter, for greasing
4 eggs
180 g (6½ oz) caster (superfine) sugar
250 g (9 oz) ground almonds
1 teaspoon baking powder
icing (confectioners') sugar, to serve

Place the orange and lemon in a saucepan, cover with water and bring to the boil. Simmer gently for 1 hour. Remove the fruit from the water, halve, remove the seeds and purée thoroughly, skin and all. Set aside to cool.

Preheat the oven to 170°C (340°F) (conventional). Lightly grease a 26 cm (10¼ in) cake tin with butter and line with baking paper.

Beat the eggs and sugar until fluffy, then mix in the citrus purée. In a bowl, combine the ground almonds and baking powder, then fold into the egg and citrus mixture. Pour the mixture into the prepared tin and bake on the middle shelf of the oven for 40–45 minutes, until golden brown and a skewer inserted into the cake comes out clean. Allow the cake to cool, then remove from the tin and serve dusted with icing sugar.

CANDIED
CITRUS PEEL

---

*Candied citrus peel, whatever the variety, but usually from the beloved Meyer lemon, was essential during my time at Chez Panisse.
Candied strips dipped in chocolate made up part of the fruit dish that was offered as a dessert. I was immediately inspired
by the method for making something so luxurious from citrus peel. Cheers to Alice Waters! Undunked and chopped, the citrus
peel is good in meringues, cakes or ice creams. It also suits casseroles with rabbit or lamb, salad dressings or fried mushrooms,
artichokes and green beans. The syrup that remains after simmering adds sophistication to cocktails, and makes a refreshing
lemonade combined with cold sparkling mineral water and a splash of lemon juice. It is also suitable for sweetening tea, desserts
or porridge, or as a topping on baked goods.*

---

8 lemons
800 g (1 lb 12 oz) sugar, plus extra for coating
200 g (7 oz) dark chocolate (at least 70% cocoa solids)

Halve the lemons, squeeze the juice into a bowl and set aside for another use. Place the lemon halves in a large saucepan, add enough cold water to cover, then bring to the boil and simmer for 10 minutes. Drain the lemon halves, return to the pan, cover again with cold water and simmer for a further 10 minutes. Repeat this step a third time, then allow the lemon halves to cool. The shells should be soft enough to pierce them easily with a knife*.

Scrape out the white pith with a spoon and cut the remaining shells into strips. Slowly heat the strips with the sugar and 400 ml (13½ fl oz) water in a saucepan, until the sugar dissolves. Simmer over low heat until the strips are almost translucent. Remove the pan from the heat and allow the citrus strips to cool a little in the syrup.

Remove the citrus strips from the syrup, spread out over a wire rack or a baking sheet lined with baking paper and leave to dry overnight. The next day, dip the strips in enough sugar to coat and store in airtight containers for up to 6 months.

Chop the chocolate and melt 70 g (2½ oz) in a bowl over a saucepan of simmering water. Add the remaining chocolate pieces to the bowl and stir until melted. Allow the chocolate to cool a little, stirring frequently. Dip the tips of the candied citrus strips in the chocolate, then lay on a sheet of baking paper to set.

---

*   With Meyer lemons, two blanching steps are often enough; with some fruit it takes four blanchings and, with grapefruit, often five. Cumquats must not be blanched at all, but rather simply sliced in rings, seeds removed and boiled in the syrup until transparent. They make a very quick accompaniment to cakes, ice cream or puddings.

CUMQUAT
RELISH

This relish is perfect over poached or grilled fish, or haloumi. If you like, stir through a handful of chopped hazelnuts or pine nuts at the end for extra crunch.

2 French shallots
pinch of salt
pinch of sugar
splash of white wine vinegar
6 cumquats
1 bunch parsley
1 handful pitted olives

Halve, peel and finely dice the shallots, then place in a bowl with the salt, sugar and vinegar. Set aside to marinate for at least 15 minutes.

Wash the cumquats under very hot water and thinly slice, removing the seeds as you go. Chop the parsley and olives. Add the cumquat, parsley and olives to the marinated shallot and mix well, adjusting the seasoning if necessary.

LEMON
MARMALADE

A Mother's Day gift from my mother-in-law, Christelle, which I tried to recreate straight away. It has been one of my favourite recipes ever since.

8 lemons
750 g (1 lb 11 oz) jam (jelly) sugar (1:1 fruit to sugar)

Thinly peel the lemons with a vegetable peeler, removing the yellow part only, then chop the peel into 5–8 mm (¼ in) dice or thin strips. Boil the peel in 1 litre (34 fl oz/4 cups) water for about 50 minutes, or until soft, then drain, reserving a little of the cooking water.

Halve and squeeze the juice from seven of the lemons. Peel away the white pith from the remaining lemon and cut the lemon segments from the membranes.

In a large saucepan, combine the boiled peel, lemon segments, lemon juice and enough reserved cooking water to total 750 ml (25½ fl oz/3 cups). Add the jam sugar and boil for about 15 minutes. Fill sterilised jars with the still-hot jam, then seal tightly.

The marmalade will keep in a cool, dark place for up to 1 year.

BITTER ORANGE
MARMALADE

The 'authentic' citrus marmalade.

---

500 g (1 lb 2 oz) bitter (Seville) oranges
500 g (1 lb 2 oz) jam (jelly) sugar (1:1 fruit to sugar)
juice of 1 lemon

Cut both ends off the bitter oranges, then halve the
oranges lengthways, remove the white fibres in the middle
and remove any seeds. Tie up the ends, seeds and white
fibres in a clean square of muslin (cheesecloth).

Very thinly slice the orange halves, then halve again, so
you have small quarter circles. Place them in a saucepan
and cover with 800 ml (27 fl oz) water. Add the muslin
bag and refrigerate overnight.

The next day, add the sugar and lemon juice to the
saucepan. Bring to the boil and reduce by half. Remove
the muslin bag, fill sterilised jars with the still-hot
marmalade and seal tightly.

The marmalade will keep in the fridge for
up to 1 year.

CURRANT TART WITH HAZELNUT MERINGUE

… that reminds me of long-ago summers.

Pastry
200 g (7 oz) plain (all-purpose) flour,
plus extra for dusting
40 g (1½ oz) caster (superfine) sugar
pinch of salt
100 g (3½ oz) cold butter
1 egg

Filling
3 tablespoons Currant jam (page 89)
250 g (9 oz) red, white or mixed
currants, plus 6–8 clusters, to garnish
160 g (5½ oz) caster (superfine) sugar
1 tablespoon cornflour (cornstarch)
3 egg whites
pinch of salt
200 g (7 oz) ground hazelnuts

Preheat the oven to 180°C (350°F) (conventional). In a large bowl,
combine the flour, sugar and salt, then rub in the butter with your
fingertips. Quickly work in the egg and knead to a smooth dough.
Roll out the pastry on a lightly floured work surface to about 5 mm
(¼ in) thick and use to line a flan (tart) tin. Refrigerate for 30 minutes.
Cover the pastry with baking paper, fill with dried beans or baking
beads and blind bake on the lowest shelf of the oven for 8–10 minutes.
Remove the paper and beans and bake the pastry for a further 5 minutes.
Allow to cool.

Spread the jam over the pastry. Strip the currants from the stalks, mix
with 1 tablespoon of the sugar and the cornflour, and scatter over the
jam. Beat the egg whites and salt to stiff peaks, add the remaining sugar
and beat for a further 1 minute. Fold in the ground hazelnuts and spread
over the currants. Bake for about 25 minutes, until golden brown.

Cool before serving and garnish with the currant clusters.

CURRANT
RELISH

Whether you spread this relish over cheese, ham or salami, serve it with antipasti, freshwater trout grilled over a wood fire, or freshly smoked Arctic char just taken out of the smokehouse, it's worth making in large quantities. During the cold season, it can bring sweet thoughts that take you back to summer.

3 red onions
1 red capsicum (bell pepper)
2 tablespoons olive oil
1 red chilli
2 cm (¾ in) piece ginger
2 garlic cloves
200 ml (7 fl oz) red wine vinegar
140 g (5 oz) sugar
pinch of Chinese five spice powder
1 teaspoon salt
200 g (7 oz) redcurrants

Peel the onions and cut into thin wedges. Wash the capsicum and finely dice. Heat the olive oil in a saucepan and sauté the onion and capsicum until soft. Halve the chilli, remove the seeds and finely chop. Peel and finely grate the ginger. Peel and finely chop the garlic. Add the chilli, ginger and garlic to the onion and capsicum, along with the vinegar, sugar, Chinese five spice and salt. Simmer over low heat for 5 minutes. Strip the currants from the stalks and add to the pan. Simmer for a further 5–10 minutes.

Fill sterilised jars with the relish, seal immediately and keep in the fridge for up to 6 months.

POPPY SEED CAKE
WITH REDCURRANTS

*You can also top this simple flourless and butterless poppy seed cake with
thinly shaved rhubarb, strawberries, apricots or grated apple.
So much variety for one little cake!*

butter or oil, for greasing
4 eggs
75 g (2¾ oz) caster (superfine) sugar
pinch of salt
75 g (2¾ oz) icing (confectioners') sugar
90 ml (3 fl oz) poppy seed oil (available from specialist stores)
50 ml (1¾ fl oz) sunflower or olive oil
200 g (7 oz) poppy seeds, ground
1 teaspoon cornflour (cornstarch)
200 g (7 oz) redcurrants

Preheat the oven to 190°C (375°F) (conventional). Lightly grease a loaf
(bar) tin with oil or butter and line with baking paper. Separate the eggs
then, using an electric mixer, beat the egg whites, caster sugar and salt
to stiff peaks. In a separate bowl, beat the egg yolks with the icing sugar
for 3–5 minutes, until creamy. Still beating, add the poppy seed and
sunflower oils in a thin stream and beat for a further 1 minute. Using a
whisk, fold in one-third of the beaten egg white, followed by the poppy
seeds, the remaining egg white and finally the cornflour. Spread the
mixture in the prepared tin. Strip the currants from the stalks (setting
a few aside for garnish) and scatter over the cake mixture.

Bake for 35–45 minutes, or until a skewer inserted into the cake comes
out clean. Allow to cool, remove from the tin and and garnish with the
reserved currants.

SUMMER FRUITS
IN LEMON VERBENA SYRUP
WITH BLACKCURRANT SORBET

*A fresh dessert that draws sophistication from its delicate sourness and light
sweetness. Served in a glass with prosecco poured over, it becomes
a wonderfully refreshing summer punch.*

Sorbet	*Marinated fruit*
250 g (9 oz) blackcurrants	250 g (9 oz) caster (superfine) sugar
150 g (5½ oz) caster (superfine) sugar	6–8 lemon verbena sprigs
½ vanilla bean	juice of ½ lemon
2 tablespoons crème de cassis (blackcurrant liqueur), plus 1–2 tablespoons extra to serve	500 g (1 lb 2 oz) mixed summer fruits (e.g. raspberries, blueberries, blackberries, redcurrants, strawberries, cherries)

For the sorbet, strip the blackcurrants from the stalks and place in a
saucepan with the sugar, vanilla bean and 500 ml (17 fl oz/2 cups)
water. Bring to the boil, stirring, until the sugar dissolves. Reduce the
heat and simmer gently for 10–15 minutes. Push the mixture through a
fine-meshed sieve into a bowl and add the crème de cassis. Allow to cool
completely. Transfer the mixture to an ice-cream machine and churn to a
sorbet according to the manufacturer's instructions.

For the marinated fruit, combine the sugar and lemon verbena in a
bowl and rub together with your hands. Place the mixture in a saucepan
with 250 ml (8½ fl oz/1 cup) water and bring to the boil, stirring, until
the sugar dissolves. Reduce the heat and simmer for 3–4 minutes, then
remove from the heat and leave to infuse for at least 20 minutes. Add
the lemon juice, then strain the mixture, discarding the solids, and
allow to cool completely. Marinate the fruit in the cooled syrup at room
temperature for at least 30 minutes.

Serve the sorbet with the marinated fruits and the extra crème de cassis.

CURRANT
CHEESECAKE

Crisp, creamy, sweet and sour all at once. Who could possibly resist?

Base
100 g (3½ oz) butter
200 g (7 oz) rich tea biscuits
(butter cookies)

Filling
1 kg (2 lb 3 oz) cream cheese
6 eggs
2 egg yolks
300 g (10½ oz) caster (superfine) sugar
pinch of salt
25 g (1 oz) plain (all-purpose) flour
120 g (4½ oz) whipped cream
scraped seeds of ½ vanilla bean
juice of 1 lemon
200 g (7 oz) blackcurrants
or redcurrants

Currant sauce
1 tablespoon caster (superfine) sugar
200 g (7 oz) blackcurrants
or redcurrants
scraped seeds of ½ vanilla bean

Preheat the oven to 180°C (350°F) (conventional). For the base, melt the butter in a saucepan over low heat. In a food processor, pulse the biscuits to fine crumbs, then pour in the butter while still processing. Push the crumb mixture into a springform cake tin lined with baking paper. Bake the biscuit base for 12–15 minutes, then remove from the oven and increase the temperature to 250°C (480°F).

For the filling, combine all the ingredients except the currants in a large bowl and mix until smooth. Spread the filling onto the pre-baked base. Strip the currants from the stalks (retaining a few for garnish) and scatter over the cream cheese mixture. Bake for 10 minutes, then reduce the temperature to 100°C (210°F). Bake the cheesecake for a further 1½ hours, turning the oven down to 60°C (140°F) for the last 15 minutes. Turn the oven off and leave the cheesecake inside to cool completely.

For the currant sauce, caramelise the sugar in a small saucepan over medium heat. Strip the currants from the stalks, then add to the sugar along with the vanilla seeds. Cook for a few minutes, until syrupy.

Garnish the cheesecake with the reserved fresh currants and serve with the currant sauce.

REDCURRANT
SORBET

*This tastes just as great on its own as it does with prosecco
or lemonade poured over. It's a wonderfully fruity refreshment
on hot summer days.*

500 g (1 lb 2 oz) redcurrants
125 ml (4 fl oz / ½ cup) redcurrant juice
180 g (6½ oz) caster (superfine) sugar
1 egg white

Strip the currants from the stalks. In a saucepan, mix
the currant juice with 150 g (5½ oz) of the sugar and
100 ml (3½ fl oz) water. Add the currants (retaining a
few for garnish) and boil for 3–4 minutes. Allow to cool,
then push the mixture through a fine-meshed sieve or
food mill into a bowl.

Using a stand mixer, beat the egg white and the
remaining sugar to stiff peaks then carefully fold into
the currant purée. Pour the mixture into an ice-cream
machine and churn according to the manufacturer's
instructions. Freeze the sorbet and the reserved currants
for about 20 minutes before serving.

VENISON CARPACCIO
WITH CURRANTS

*Another souvenir from a holiday in Sweden. By the way, left-over radish leaves add a wonderful
peppery note to this dish. If you like, spread a few leaves over the carpaccio, then drizzle with olive oil
and season with salt and a little pepper before serving. You can also use beef (Scotch) fillet if venison is unavailable.*

200 g (7 oz) venison backstrap
1 small bunch mixed fresh herbs
(e.g. parsley, chervil, thyme, rosemary)
fleur de sel and coarsely ground black pepper
1 teaspoon olive oil, plus extra to serve
1 small red onion

1 handful redcurrants
1 thyme sprig
1 tablespoon honey
2–3 radishes
10 g (⅓ oz) shaved parmesan

Remove the venison from the fridge 1 hour before you begin. Finely chop the herbs and spread on a plate. Roll the venison in the herbs, then season with fleur de sel and pepper.

Heat a heavy-based frying pan over high heat. Add the olive oil and sear the venison for about 10 seconds on all sides – the top and bottom should be evenly coloured but only slightly at the edges; the inside should still be rare. Remove from the pan and allow to cool.

Slice the venison as thinly as possible using a very sharp knife. Lay plastic wrap on a clean work surface, then spread out the venison slices with a 3 cm (1¼ in) gap in between them (you may need to do this in batches). Cover with a second sheet of plastic wrap and, using a rolling pin, roll the meat even thinner.

Peel the onion and shave very thinly using a mandoline. Strip the currants from the stalks and pick the thyme leaves. Combine the onion and currants with the honey in a small saucepan and simmer gently for 3–5 minutes. Add the thyme and season with fleur de sel and pepper. Thinly shave the radishes.

Arrange the venison slices on plates or a platter. Top with the radish slices and spoon over the onion and currant mixture. Season with fleur de sel and pepper, and serve garnished with the shaved parmesan and a drizzle of olive oil.

CURRANT
JAM

*Sweet and sour at the same time, this jam improves
cakes or stews and is also a true treat enjoyed with
bread and butter.*

1 kg (2 lb 3 oz) redcurrants
500 g (1 lb 2 oz) jam (jelly) sugar (2:1 fruit to sugar)
juice of ½ lemon

Strip the currants from the stalks and heat in
a saucepan with the sugar and lemon juice, stirring
constantly. Boil for 6–8 minutes.

Pass the jam through a food mill. Fill sterilised jars
with the still-hot jam and seal tightly.

The jam will keep in the fridge for 1 year.

E

ELDERBERRIES

ELDERFLOWER ICE CREAM

For me, elderflowers taste like a beautiful edible perfume!
Here, they give ice cream a gorgeous flowery touch.

250 ml (8½ fl oz / 1 cup) milk
120 g (4½ oz) sugar
6 egg yolks
scraped seeds of ½ vanilla bean
pinch of salt
500 ml (17 fl oz / 2 cups) whipped cream
20 elderflower blossoms

In a saucepan, heat the milk, sugar, egg yolks, vanilla
and salt over low heat, stirring constantly, until the cream
begins to thicken. Place the whipped cream in a bowl
and pour over the thickened cream mixture: this will
immediately stop the cream cooking. Stir through the
elderflower blossoms, then cover and refrigerate for
1–2 days.

Pass the elderflower cream through a sieve, then churn
in an ice-cream machine according to the manufacturer's
instructions. Serve immediately.

ELDERBERRY JAM

Whether you use it to accompany sweet dumplings or cream cheese, or as a special ingredient in a game stew, venison carpaccio or ham, there's probably no jam more flexible.

1 kg (2 lb 3 oz) elderberry clusters
500 g (1 lb 2 oz) jam (jelly) sugar (2:1 fruit to sugar)

Pick the elderberries from the stalks and bring to the boil in a large saucepan with the sugar and 3 tablespoons water. Boil for about 5–8 minutes, stirring occasionally.

As soon as the elderberries release their juice, remove the pan from the heat and pass the berries through a food mill. Fill sterilised jars with the still-hot jam and seal tightly.

The jam will keep in the fridge for 1 year.

FRIED
ELDERFLOWERS

*Freshly fried elderflowers lightly dusted with icing sugar are
the pure taste of spring. Instead of beer, wine or sparkling
mineral water also work well.*

130 g (4½ oz) plain (all-purpose) flour
large pinch of salt
2 tablespoons caster (superfine) sugar
2 eggs
220 ml (7½ fl oz) pale lager
500 ml (17 fl oz/2 cups) sunflower oil, for frying
16–20 elderflower clusters
icing (confectioners') sugar, for dusting

In a bowl, mix the flour, salt, sugar and eggs until
smooth. Gradually add the beer, ensuring the batter
remains smooth.

Heat the sunflower oil in a deep frying pan or small
saucepan. Test the temperature of the oil with the handle
of a wooden spoon: when small bubbles form around the
handle, the oil is hot enough. Working with one cluster at
a time, hold the elderflowers by the stem and drag them
through the batter. Fry the cluster in the oil until golden,
turning once if necessary, then drain on paper towel.
Serve dusted with icing sugar.

ELDERBERRY CAPERS

*Unripened green elderberries pickle really well
and can be used just like capers.*

12–15 elderberry clusters with green berries
coarse sea salt
100 ml (3½ fl oz) white wine vinegar
1 teaspoon sugar
1 tarragon sprig
1 bay leaf

Pick the elderberries from the stalks and place in a
sealable jar. Cover with sea salt, seal the jar and leave
overnight. Remove the berries and salt from the jar, and
set aside 1 tablespoon of the residual liquid. Boil the
berries in water for 5 minutes, then rinse with cold water.

Heat the vinegar and sugar in a small saucepan until
the sugar dissolves. Thoroughly clean the jar with hot
water, then fill it with the tarragon, bay leaf, elderberries,
vinegar and sugar mixture and the reserved 1 tablespoon
liquid. Top up with boiling water and seal. Allow to cool
and leave in a cool place for a few weeks to develop.

The elderberry capers will keep in the fridge for up to
1 year.

ELDERFLOWER
VINEGAR

A Mum-in-law classic!

10 elderflower clusters (without stalks)
1 litre (34 fl oz/4 cups) white wine vinegar
or white balsamic vinegar
2 cloves

Fill a large sterilised jar with all the ingredients, cover
the top with a piece of muslin (cheesecloth) and fasten
with an elastic band. Leave in a warm place and shake
carefully every 1–2 days.

After about 14 days, strain the vinegar and transfer
to sterilised bottles.

The vinegar will keep in a cool, dark place for
up to 1 year.

ELDERFLOWER CORDIAL

And yet another mother-in-law recipe.
Drinking elderflower cordial reminds me of summer,
wandering the fields, woods and meadows,
doing silly things and being a child again.

2 kg (4 lb 6 oz) sugar
3–4 lemons
30 elderflower clusters (without stalks)
2 tablespoons citric acid

In a large saucepan or stockpot, bring 2 litres
(68 fl oz/8 cups) water and the sugar to the boil. Reduce
the heat and simmer until the sugar dissolves. Remove
from the heat and allow to cool.

Slice the lemons and add to the sugar syrup, along with
the elderflowers and citric acid. Leave in a cool place for
2–3 days, stirring once a day. Pour into sterilised jars or
bottles and seal well.

The syrup will keep in the fridge for a maximum
of 6 months.

ELDERBERRY PURÉE

*As children, we often used to eat elderberry purée with
creamy polenta or semolina. Sometimes we had it with
shredded pancakes or semolina dumplings, or simply cold,
eaten as stewed fruit with a spoonful of sour cream.*

4–5 damsons
1 pear
1 apple
250 ml (8½ fl oz / 1 cup) apple juice or water
500 g (1 lb 2 oz) ripe elderberries, picked
100 g (3½ oz) sugar
1 cinnamon stick
1 clove
1 strip lemon zest
1 tablespoon cornflour (cornstarch)

Halve the damsons, discard the stones and cut into cubes.
Peel, halve and core the pear and apple, and cut
into cubes.

In a saucepan, combine the fruit with 190 ml
(6½ fl oz) of the apple juice, the elderberries, sugar,
cinnamon stick, clove and lemon zest. Bring to the boil,
then simmer over low heat for 10–15 minutes. Mix the
cornflour with the remaining apple juice until smooth,
then add to the stewed elderberries and return to the boil.

Remove from the heat and store in sterilised jars.

VENISON RAGOUT WITH ELDERBERRIES
AND SCHUPFNUDELN

When the days become shorter and cooler, we often start craving warming stews. Elderberries provide a real sourness to this dish, plus they look beautiful, too.

Ragout

800 g (1 lb 12 oz) venison shoulder

3–4 cm (1¼–1½ in) piece ginger

2 garlic cloves

250 g (9 oz) French shallots

olive oil, for frying

3 tablespoons tomato paste (concentrated purée)

3 tablespoons Elderberry jam (jelly) (page 93), or Apple or Quince jam (page 179)

1 cinnamon stick

1 star anise

2 cloves

3 juniper berries, lightly crushed

3 whole allspice berries

½ teaspoon coriander seeds

½ teaspoon fennel seeds

2 thyme sprigs

500 ml (17 fl oz/2 cups) strong red wine

500 ml (17 fl oz/2 cups) game or chicken stock

1 small red kuri pumpkin (winter squash)

200 g (7 oz) ripe elderberries, picked

1 square bittersweet dark chocolate

250 ml (8½ fl oz/1 cup) espresso coffee

1 tablespoon finely grated orange zest

1 tablespoon balsamic vinegar

½–1 tablespoon cornflour (cornstarch) (optional)

salt and freshly ground black pepper, to taste

Schupfnudeln

500 g (1 lb 2 oz) roasting potatoes

140 g (5 oz) plain (all-purpose) flour, plus extra for dusting

50 g (1¾ oz) quark

1 egg

freshly grated nutmeg, to taste

To finish

2–3 tablespoons butter

2 tablespoons poppy seeds, finely crushed

Cut the meat into 4 × 4 cm (1½ × 1½ in) dice. Peel the ginger and garlic and finely chop. Peel the shallots and cut into quarters.

Preheat the oven to 150°C (300°F) (conventional). Heat a flameproof casserole dish on the stovetop and add a little olive oil. Working in batches, brown the meat on all sides, ensuring that the meat has plenty of room and doesn't begin to boil rather than fry. Transfer the meat to a plate or tray and set aside.

In the same dish, briefly fry the shallot, garlic and ginger, then add the tomato paste, jam or jelly, spices and thyme. Return the venison to the dish and pour in the wine and stock. Briefly bring to the boil, then transfer to the lowest shelf of the oven and cook for 2½ hours until the meat is tender and juicy.

Meanwhile, halve the pumpkin, remove the seeds with a spoon and cut the flesh into 3 cm (1¼ in) wide wedges. Add the pumpkin wedges and elderberries to the stew about 45 minutes before the end of cooking. At the end of cooking, stir in the chocolate, coffee, orange zest and vinegar. If the sauce is a little thin for your liking, mix the cornflour with a little cold water, then stir into the sauce. Season the stew with salt and pepper.

For the schupfnudeln, peel the potatoes and boil in salted water until soft. Drain, then return the potato to the saucepan and set over the switched-off stovetop to dry off the excess moisture. Press the potatoes through a potato ricer and work in the remaining ingredients to form a supple dough. Add a little more flour if the dough is too moist to be shaped.

On a well-dusted work surface, roll one-quarter of the dough into a long sausage about 1 cm (½ in) thick. Cut into 3 cm (1¼ in) lengths and, using flour-dusted hands, shape the ends into points. Repeat until all the dough has been shaped. Bring plenty of lightly salted water to the boil. Working in batches, add the schupfnudeln, removing them with a skimmer or slotted spoon as they rise to the surface. Drain well. Melt the butter in a non-stick frying pan, add the poppy seeds, then toss through the drained schupfnudeln a few times.

Share the ragout among plates and top with the schupfnudeln.

F

FIGS

GLAZED QUAIL WITH FIGS
AND PISTACHIO COUSCOUS

This was the first quail recipe I wrote after I started cooking professionally.
Matching them with figs just felt good somehow – and I was right. A dream duo!

Glazed quail
6 slices sandwich bread
4 quails
½ teaspoon salt
½ teaspoon pepper
100 g (3½ oz) butter
3 teaspoons honey
3 tablespoons Bitter orange marmalade (page 79)
4–5 French shallots
50 ml (1¾ fl oz) port
200 ml (7 fl oz) chicken stock
2–3 sage sprigs
4–6 fresh figs

Pistachio couscous
200 g (7 oz) couscous
pinch of salt, plus extra to taste
½ teaspoon ras el hanout
1 tablespoon olive oil
juice of ½ orange
1 handful shelled green pistachios
1 handful coriander (cilantro) leaves
1 handful mint leaves
freshly ground black pepper, to taste

Preheat the oven to 200°C (400°F) (conventional). Cut the bread into cubes. Stuff the breast cavities of the quails with the bread and truss the legs with kitchen twine. Place the quails in an ovenproof frying pan and season with the salt and pepper.

In a small saucepan, melt the butter, honey and marmalade and brush the quails thoroughly with this mixture. Peel and halve the shallots and add to the quail pan. Add the port, stock and sage. Roast for 10–15 minutes, basting regularly with the liquid in the pan.

Carefully remove the hot pan from the oven and place on the stovetop over low heat. Halve the figs and add to the pan. Cook, turning the quails frequently, until they are nicely browned and covered with the glaze.

Meanwhile, make the pistachio couscous. In a large bowl, combine the couscous, pinch of salt, ras el hanout, olive oil and orange juice. Add boiling water to about 1 cm (½ in) above the grains. Mix well once, then cover and leave for 10 minutes to swell up. Carefully fluff up the couscous with a fork and allow to cool. Roughly chop the pistachios, coriander and mint, then fold into the couscous and season with salt and pepper.

Spoon the couscous onto plates and top with the quail and fig mixture.

FIG LEAF ICE CREAM

Fig leaves have the most beautiful scent. Their smell and taste are reminiscent of coconut palms – heaven! This ice cream is perfect with fresh or grilled figs*.

250 ml (8½ fl oz/1 cup) milk
150 g (5½ oz) caster (superfine) sugar
6 egg yolks
pinch of salt
500 ml (17 fl oz/2 cups) thickened (whipping) cream
4–6 fresh fig leaves

In a saucepan, warm the milk, sugar, egg yolks and salt over low heat, stirring constantly, until the mixture gradually begins to thicken. Pour the cream into a bowl and add the warmed milk and egg yolk mixture – this stops the cooking process straight away. Place the fig leaves in the ice-cream mixture and refrigerate for 5–6 hours or overnight to infuse. Strain the mixture, then churn in an ice-cream maker according to the manufacturer's instructions.

* A few fresh or grilled figs taste unbelievably good with this! To grill figs, halve them, drizzle with a few drops of olive oil and cook in a chargrill pan or on a grill plate for 3–4 minutes. Turn the figs over, grill for a further 1 minute, drizzle over 1 teaspoon honey and a few splashes of balsamic vinegar, and serve with the ice cream.

FIG
CHUTNEY

*This is especially good with soft goat's cheese on Fruit bread (page 153),
or with blue cheese or pecorino.*

10–12 figs
1 red onion
2 tablespoons olive oil
3 tablespoons soft brown sugar
1 teaspoon mustard seeds
4 thyme sprigs
60 ml (2 fl oz/¼ cup) white balsamic vinegar
juice of ½ lemon
salt and freshly ground black pepper, to taste

Cut the figs into wedges. Peel and halve the onion, then thinly slice. Heat
the olive oil in a saucepan and sauté the onion, stirring frequently, until
translucent. Add the sugar and lightly caremelise the onion. Add the figs,
mustard seeds and thyme and, stirring constantly, cook for 4 minutes.
Deglaze with the balsamic vinegar and 60 ml (2 fl oz/¼ cup) water.

Simmer the mixture over low heat for 15–20 minutes, stirring
occasionally. Add the lemon juice, season with salt and pepper, then pour
into sterilised jars while still hot and seal well.

The chutney will keep in the fridge for a maximum of 6 months.

GRILLED FIGS
WITH PROSCIUTTO

Like an old glove, but for me never out of fashion.

4 figs
1–2 tablespoons olive oil, plus extra for frying
200 g (7 oz) sliceable soft cheese
(such as Baked ricotta, page 185)
250 ml (8½ fl oz/1 cup) canola oil
1 handful purple sage leaves
salt, to taste
4 slices prosciutto
freshly ground black pepper, to taste
2–3 tablespoons balsamic vinegar
small piece honeycomb or a few teaspoons honey, to serve

Halve the figs and place, cut side down, in a chargrill pan with the extra olive oil. Grill until dark brown. Slice the cheese. Heat the canola oil in a small, deep saucepan. Test the temperature of the oil with the handle of a wooden spoon: when small bubbles form around the handle, the oil is hot enough. Drop the sage leaves into the oil and fry for 1–2 minutes until crisp. Remove with a skimmer or slotted spoon, then drain on paper towel and season with salt.

Divide the figs among plates and arrange the cheese, prosciutto and sage leaves on top. Season with pepper. Drizzle over the balsamic vinegar and olive oil, and serve with a piece of honeycomb or a drizzle of honey.

If you like, serve this with a salad of rocket (arugula),
beetroot (beet) leaves and wild herbs.

G

GOOSEBERRIES, GRAPES

CREPES WITH QUARK CREAM AND GOOSEBERRIES

Palatschinken (what we in Austria call very thin pancakes) have accompanied me all my life.
I like them best the classic way, with apricot jam (jelly) or grilled cheese. Besides sweet and sour gooseberries,
you can try any other fully ripe fruit imaginable.

Crepes	*Quark cream*	*Stewed gooseberries*
25 g (1 oz) butter, plus extra for frying	1 lemon	25 g (1 oz) butter
125 g (4½ oz) plain (all-purpose) flour	120 g (4½ oz) caster	1 tablespoon caster (superfine) sugar
pinch of salt	(superfine) sugar	1 orange
1 tablespoon caster (superfine) sugar	scraped seeds of ½ vanilla bean	200 g (7 oz) gooseberries
2 eggs	2 eggs	1 teaspoon orange-flavoured liqueur
250 ml (8½ fl oz/1 cup) milk	100 g (3½ oz) very cold butter	
50 ml (1¾ fl oz) sparkling	250 g (9 oz) quark	*To serve*
mineral water		icing (confectioners') sugar
1 teaspoon orange-flavoured liqueur		

For the crepes, melt the butter. In a large bowl, mix the flour, salt and sugar. Add the eggs and whisk to a smooth batter. Gradually add the milk and melted butter, whisking until smooth. Add the mineral water and orange liqueur. Cover the batter and leave to rest for 1 hour.

For the quark cream, grate ½ teaspoon zest from the lemon, then squeeze the juice. Combine the lemon zest and juice, sugar, vanilla seeds and eggs in a saucepan over low heat. Stirring constantly, gently allow to thicken for 8–10 minutes. Cut the butter into small cubes and stir into the egg mixture, one cube at a time, until all the butter has been used. Transfer to a bowl and allow to cool. Add the quark, stir until smooth, then cover and chill for at least 1 hour.

For the stewed gooseberries, melt the butter in a frying pan, then add the sugar and caramelise until golden. Grate ½ teaspoon zest from the orange, then squeeze the juice. Add the gooseberries, orange zest and juice and orange liqueur to the pan, and simmer for 2–3 minutes. Remove from the heat and allow to cool.

Preheat the oven to 100°C (210°F) (conventional). To cook the crepes, heat 1 teaspoon butter in a non-stick frying pan and fry a test pancake. From now on you can dispense with the butter. Cook thin crepes, one at a time, over medium heat. Keep the cooked crepes warm in the oven.

Spread 2 tablespoons of the quark cream on each crepe and place the stewed gooseberries on top. Roll up the crepes and serve dusted with icing sugar.

PORT-BRAISED VEAL CHEEKS
WITH GOOSEBERRIES AND CHANTERELLES

Butter-soft veal cheeks, braised in a delicate sweet sauce, pair perfectly with sour gooseberries. This dish goes really well with creamy polenta, or potato or celeriac mash.

10–12 veal cheeks
50 g (1¾ oz) soft brown sugar
500 ml (17 fl oz/2 cups) vegetable or chicken stock
100 ml (3½ fl oz) balsamic vinegar
250 ml (8½ fl oz/1 cup) port
100 ml (3½ fl oz) orange juice
5 garlic cloves
6 French shallots

3 cm (1¼ in) piece ginger
olive oil, for frying
2 red chillies
2 bay leaves
2 cloves
1 cinnamon stick
8 juniper berries
1 star anise
200 g (7 oz) gooseberries

splash red wine vinegar
100 g (3½ oz) small chanterelles
salt and freshly ground black pepper, to taste
2–3 sprigs each of tarragon, mint and lovage
1 tablespoon potato starch

Wash the veal cheeks and pat dry with paper towel. Make a marinade by caramelising the sugar in a small saucepan until dark brown. Pour in the stock, balsamic vinegar, port and orange juice, then simmer until the sugar dissolves. Peel and thinly slice the garlic and five of the shallots. Peel and finely chop or grate the ginger.

Heat a little olive oil in a frying pan and sauté the garlic, sliced shallot and ginger for 5–10 minutes. Add to the marinade. Halve and deseed the chillies, and finely chop. Add the chilli, bay leaves and spices to the marinade and allow to cool. Pour the marinade over the veal and marinate in the fridge for at least 3 hours.

Preheat the oven to 150°C (300°F) (conventional). Remove the veal cheeks from the marinade and pat dry. Heat a flameproof casserole dish on the stovetop, add some olive oil and sear the veal cheeks all over for 2–3 minutes, then add the marinade. Add half the gooseberries, then transfer to the oven and braise for 2½–3 hours, or until the meat is tender.

Peel the remaining shallot, then slice into thin rings. Heat a little olive oil in a frying pan and briefly sauté the shallot. Add the red wine vinegar, then transfer to a bowl and set aside. Wipe the pan clean with paper towel. Clean the chanterelles and heat a little more olive oil in the frying pan over high heat. Add the chanterelles and sear briefly. Season with salt and pepper, then add to the shallot. Halve the remaining gooseberries and pick the tarragon, mint and lovage leaves. Add to the chanterelles and shallot, along with 1 tablespoon olive oil.

Remove the veal cheeks from the oven. Mix the potato starch with a little cold water until smooth, then quickly stir into the stew. Return the dish to the stovetop and cook over high heat until the sauce has thickened. Serve the veal and sauce with the marinated gooseberries and chanterelles.

CRISPY MACKEREL WITH
SWEET-AND-SOUR GOOSEBERRIES

Buttery tender fish and sweet-and-sour fruit couldn't be enjoyed in a better way.
This recipe's for my editor!

Pickled gooseberries	Mackerel	Dressing	Herb salad
150 g (5½ oz) gooseberries	4 mackerel fillets	1½ tablespoons gooseberry	1 handful nasturtium leaves
1 French shallot	2 tablespoons vermouth	pickling liquid (from the	1 handful herbs (e.g. mint,
3 teaspoons sugar	salt, for seasoning	pickled gooseberries)	tarragon, parsley,
60–75 ml (2–2¾ fl oz)	olive oil, for brushing	3 tablespoons olive oil	coriander/cilantro …)
apple cider vinegar		juice of 1 orange	
1 oregano sprig		1 teaspoon ground cumin	

For the pickled gooseberries, halve the gooseberries. Peel the shallot and shave thinly using a mandoline. In a small saucepan, bring the sugar and vinegar to the boil, and cook until the sugar dissolves. Add the gooseberries, shallot and oregano, then cover and marinate for at least 30 minutes or even overnight.

For the mackerel, preheat the oven to 200°C (400°F) (conventional). Pour the vermouth into a shallow bowl. Wash the mackerel fillets under cold water, then drag them through the vermouth. Season the mackerel with salt on both sides and leave at room temperature for 20 minutes.

Line a baking tray with baking paper and brush the paper lightly with olive oil. Pat the fish dry with paper towel and lay, skin side up, on the prepared tray. Lightly brush the skin of the mackerel with olive oil. Cook in the oven for 8–12 minutes.

For the dressing, place all the ingredients in a jar. Seal tightly and shake well to combine.

For the herb salad, mix the nasturtium and herbs in a bowl and toss in the dressing.

Serve the mackerel with the pickled gooseberries and the herb salad.

GOOSEBERRY
MERINGUE PIE

Sweet meringue meets acidic fruit. Nothing more is needed.

Pastry
100 g (3½ oz) butter
200 g (7 oz) plain (all-purpose) flour,
plus extra for dusting
2 tablespoons caster (superfine) sugar
pinch of salt
1 egg

Lemon filling
250 g (9 oz) cold butter
3 eggs
3 egg yolks
85 g (3 oz) caster (superfine) sugar
1 teaspoon orange-flavoured liqueur
finely grated zest and juice of
4 lemons
pinch of orange zest

Fruit topping
500 g (1 lb 2 oz) gooseberries

Meringue
70 g (2½ oz) icing (confectioners') sugar
70 g (2½ oz) caster (superfine) sugar
70 g (2½ oz) egg white (from about
2 medium eggs)
pinch of salt

Preheat the oven to 180°C (350°F) (conventional). For the pastry, in a large bowl, rub the butter into the flour, sugar and salt using your fingertips. Quickly work in the egg and knead to a smooth dough. Wrap in plastic wrap and refrigerate for 30 minutes.

Roll the pastry out on a floured work surface to 3–4 mm (⅛ in) thick circle. Line a flan (tart) tin with the pastry. Cover the pastry with baking paper, fill with dried beans or baking beads and blind bake for 8–10 minutes. Remove the paper and beans and bake the pastry for a further 5 minutes. Allow to cool.

For the lemon filling, cut the cold butter into cubes. Combine the eggs, egg yolks, sugar, orange liqueur, lemon zest and juice and orange zest in a saucepan and beat with a whisk. Warm over low heat, whisking constantly, and gradually add the butter one cube at a time. Whisk for 10–15 minutes over low heat, until the

mixture begins to thicken. Remove the pan from the heat and strain the liquid. Spread the lemon mixture over the tart base and allow to cool.

For the topping, halve the gooseberries and arrange on the lemon filling.

For the meringue, fill a small saucepan one-third full with water and place over low heat. Combine all the ingredients in the bowl of a stand mixer, then place the bowl over the saucepan. Stir well until the mixture turns pale and becomes lukewarm, and the sugar is well dissolved. Transfer the bowl to the mixer and beat for about 5 minutes, until the meringue is shiny and forms stiff peaks. Using a piping bag fitted with a plain nozzle, pipe small dollops of meringue over the tart. Bake for 8–10 minutes, until the meringue tips are nicely brown.

RICOTTA
WITH MARINATED GRAPES

*… or breakfast in Apulia, where every morning on our honeymoon
I enjoyed ricotta with fruit and honey. I admit it's not easy to find
really good ricotta made purely from whey, but it's worth seeking out!
This recipe also works, however, with Greek-style yoghurt.*

400 g (14 oz) ricotta
½ vanilla bean
200 ml (7 fl oz) dessert wine
1 lemon verbena sprig
2 bay leaves

1 strip lemon zest
200 g (7 oz) grapes
1 handful sultanas (golden raisins)
4 slices brioche

Drain the ricotta in a clean square of muslin (cheesecloth). Tie up the
corners to create a bag and sit the wrapped ricotta in a sieve or colander
set over a bowl. Weigh down the ricotta with a plate and leave overnight
in the fridge.

Split the vanilla bean lengthways and scrape out the seeds.
In a saucepan, combine the dessert wine with the vanilla seeds and
bean, lemon verbena, bay leaves and lemon zest and bring to the boil.
Reduce the heat and simmer for 15–20 minutes, until reduced by one-
third. Allow the mixture to cool a little, then add the grapes and sultanas.
Leave to marinate until cold.

Toast the brioche, then spread with the ricotta and spoon the grapes and
sultanas, along with the sauce, over the top.

AJO BLANCO WITH GRAPES
AND GRAPESEED OIL

*Through roasting in the oven, garlic becomes pleasantly sweet and soft and
loses its strong peppery taste. Each clove pops so easily out of its skin.
Perfect for a hot summer's day!*

1 garlic bulb
200 g (7 oz) blanched almonds
200 g (7 oz) ciabatta
1 litre (34 fl oz/4 cups) vegetable stock or water
1 white onion
1 tablespoon olive oil
¼ teaspoon ground cumin
¼ teaspoon ground coriander
4 teaspoons sherry or white-wine vinegar
125 ml (4 fl oz/½ cup) orange juice
salt and freshly ground black pepper, to taste
1 bunch seedless muscat grapes
grapeseed oil, for drizzling

Preheat the oven to 180°C (350°F) (conventional). Wrap the garlic bulb
in foil and roast for 30–40 minutes. Allow the garlic to cool a little, then
squeeze the garlic purée from the cloves.

Meanwhile, toast the almonds in the oven for 8–10 minutes. Tear the
bread into chunks and soak in the stock or water. Peel and finely chop
the onion, then sauté in the olive oil for 5–8 minutes, until soft and
caramelised. Transfer the onion to a blender, along with the garlic,
soaked bread and stock and the remaining ingredients except the grapes
and grapeseed oil. Purée until smooth, then refrigerate.

Serve the soup cold, garnished with the grapes and a drizzle
of grapeseed oil.

ZANDER ON ROAST GRAPES WITH LENTILS AND BRUSSELS SPROUTS

When roasted, the grapes in this dish lose their natural sugars to the sauce, leaving behind a mild caramel flavour that lightly coats the brussels sprouts and the lentils. It all goes fantastically well with zander or Arctic char.

Lentils and vegetables
1 French shallot
1 celery stalk
1 tablespoon butter
1 garlic clove
½ teaspoon bread spices (available from specialist stores)
1 bay leaf
3–4 thyme sprigs
200 g (7 oz) beluga lentils
125 ml (4 fl oz / ½ cup) dry white wine

2 tablespoons balsamic vinegar
1 tablespoon soy sauce
salt and freshly ground black pepper, to taste
250 g (9 oz) grapes
200 g (7 oz) brussels sprouts
2 tablespoons olive oil
½ bunch parsley

Fish
softened butter, for greasing
600 g (1 lb 5 oz) skinless zander, Arctic char or trout fillets
4 teaspoons capers, rinsed and squeezed dry
2 teaspoons finely grated lemon zest
juice of 1 lemon
splash of white wine
1 tablespoon olive oil
4–8 slices lardo

For the lentils and vegetables, peel and finely dice the shallot and celery. Melt the butter in a large saucepan, then sauté the shallot and celery for a few minutes until translucent. Peel and finely chop the garlic, then add to the pan, along with the bread spices, bay leaf, 1–2 thyme sprigs and the lentils. Pour in the wine, then add enough water to cover and simmer for 20–25 minutes, until the lentils are soft. To finish, add the balsamic vinegar and soy sauce, and season with salt and pepper.

Preheat the oven to 200°C (400°F) (conventional). Pick the grapes from the stalks. Clean the brussels sprouts, removing the outer leaves if necessary, then blanch for 2 minutes in boiling salted water. Plunge immediately into cold water and leave to drain. In a roasting tin lined with baking paper, mix the grapes and brussels sprouts with the olive oil, the remaining thyme sprigs

and a sprinkling of salt. Roast for 15–20 minutes. Chop the parsley, then fold through the lentils, along with the grapes and brussels sprouts. Season to taste with salt and pepper.

For the fish, reduce the oven temperature to 120°C (250°F). Grease an ovenproof dish with the softened butter, and lay the zander fillets on top. Arrange the capers, lemon zest and juice, wine, olive oil and lardo on top and season with salt and pepper. Cook the fish on the middle shelf of the oven for 10–15 minutes, until tender.

Reheat the lentils if necessary, then divide among plates. Top with the fish, capers and lardo, and drizzle over the cooking juices.

VERJUICE

*Verjuice or 'green juice' is obtained
from unripe grapes, and can be used to
add gentle sourness anywhere you would
otherwise use lemon juice or vinegar.
I love verjuice in soft drinks
or aperitifs.*

4–5 bunches unripe grapes

Squeeze the juice from the grapes into
a saucepan and gently heat for
10 minutes. Strain the juice through
a fine-meshed sieve or a colander
lined with muslin (cheesecloth).

Pour the still-hot juice into sterilised
bottles and seal well.

The verjuice will keep in the fridge
for a few weeks.

FRANGIPANE TART WITH GRAPES ON THE VINE

This delicious tart tastes wonderful with every imaginable fruit I can find.
A spoonful of crème fraîche or a scoop of ice cream always goes perfectly.

Pastry
1 tablespoon rosemary leaves
200 g (7 oz) wholemeal (whole-wheat) flour, plus extra for dusting
1 teaspoon caster (superfine) sugar
pinch of salt
100 g (3½ oz) cold butter
1 egg
splash of milk

Almond cream
100 g (3½ oz) butter, softened
2 tablespoons caster (superfine) sugar
scraped seeds of ½ vanilla bean
pinch of salt
1 egg, lightly beaten
100 g (3½ oz) ground almonds
2 teaspoons plain (all-purpose) flour
4 teaspoons amaretto or orange-flavoured liqueur
½ teaspoon finely grated lemon zest

Garnish
200 g (7 oz) green, red or mixed grapes, stalks attached

For the pastry, finely chop the rosemary leaves. Place the leaves in a large bowl and add the flour, sugar and salt. Cut the butter into small cubes, then rub into the flour mixture with your fingertips. Add the egg and milk and quickly mix everything to form a smooth dough. Wrap in plastic wrap and refrigerate for 30 minutes.

Preheat the oven to 180°C (350°F) (conventional). Roll out the pastry on a well-floured work surface to a 2–3 mm (⅛ in) thick rectangle. Line a rectangular flan (tart) tin with the pastry. Cover the pastry with baking paper, fill with dried beans or baking beads and blind bake on the lowest shelf of the oven for 8–10 minutes. Remove the paper and beans and bake the pastry for a further 5 minutes. Remove the pastry from the oven and allow to cool.

Meanwhile, make the almond cream. In a stand mixer fitted with a whisk attachment, beat the butter, sugar, vanilla seeds and salt until pale and fluffy. Fold in the egg. In a small bowl, mix the ground almonds and flour then fold into the cream mixture. To finish, fold in the amaretto or orange liqueur and the lemon zest.

Spread the almond cream over the pastry. Pick the majority of the grapes from the stalks and arrange over the cream. Finish by garnishing with a few grape clusters.

Reduce the oven temperature to 170°C (340°F) and bake the tart on the middle shelf for 35–40 minutes. Allow to cool a little before serving.

Frangipane tart with grapes on the vine

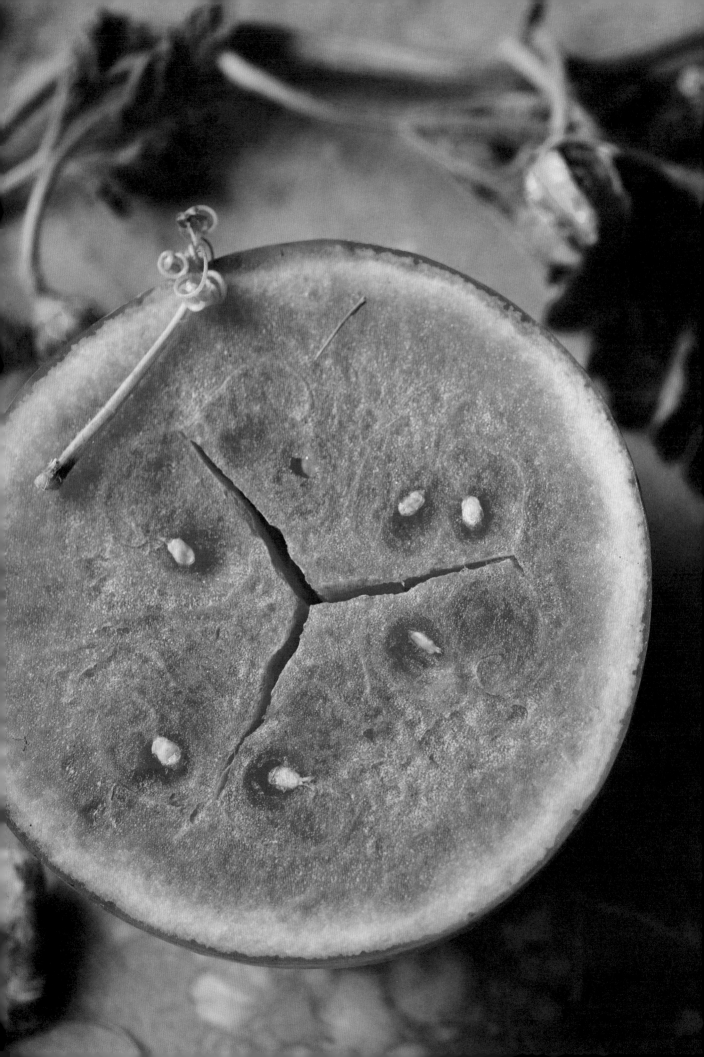

M

MELONS

MELON GAZPACHO

A melon should always be part of a day at the beach! My favourite way to eat them is on their own, in wedges, and to wash my melon-smeared face afterwards in the salt water. This refreshing gazpacho with yoghurt is best drunk or eaten cold, and cools you down on summer days when there's no sea nearby.

1 honeydew melon or rockmelon (cantaloupe)
1 tarragon sprig
1 basil sprig
2 tablespoons Greek-style yoghurt, plus extra to serve
1 tablespoon olive oil, plus extra to serve
1 slice white bread (I used ¼ focaccia), crusts removed
500 ml (17 fl oz/2 cups) cold vegetable stock
1 teaspoon white-wine vinegar
1 teaspoon salt
pinch of sweet paprika, for garnish

Halve the melon, remove the seeds with a spoon and scrape the flesh from the rind. Place the flesh in a blender. Pick the tarragon and basil leaves and add to the blender, along with the remaining ingredients except the paprika. Purée thoroughly, then refrigerate until ready to serve.

Divide the gazpacho among small bowls or the hollowed-out melon halves and drizzle over a little extra yoghurt (loosened with a few drops of milk if necessary) and extra olive oil. To finish, sprinkle with the paprika.

WATERMELON
ICE BLOCKS

For me, freezing watermelons tickles more sweetness out of them. If you freeze this mixture in a larger container, you'll quickly have a wonderful sorbet as a palate cleanser or dessert.

1 small seedless watermelon
6–8 ice-block (popsicle/ice lolly) moulds or plastic cups
6–8 wooden ice block (popsicle/ice lolly) sticks

Halve the watermelon and very thinly shave 6–8 slices from one half. Using a spoon, scrape the remaining melon flesh from the rind and purée in a blender. Place a watermelon slice in each ice-block mould and pour the purée over the top. Place the moulds in the freezer. When the purée is half frozen, insert the sticks. Freeze overnight.

Dip the moulds briefly in warm water before removing the ice blocks.

PROSCIUTTO AND
MELON

*A classic, and should remain so.
The breath-thin, sweet melon slices,
nestled with the salty prosciutto,
brings great refinement to this dish.*

1 rockmelon (cantaloupe)
150 g (5½ oz) prosciutto slices
2–3 micro basil sprigs (if possible, with flowers)
olive oil, for drizzling
fleur de sel and freshly ground black pepper,
to taste

Halve the rockmelon, remove the seeds and
cut into wedges. Remove and discard the skin,
then, using a mandoline, shave the flesh as thinly
as possible.

Arrange on a platter with the prosciutto. Pick the
basil leaves and flowers. Drizzle the prosciutto
and melon with olive oil, top with the basil and
season with fleur de sel and pepper.

MELON
WITH ICE CREAM

*Fast, simple and not just
for children's birthdays.*

1 small canary melon
4–6 scoops Vanilla ice cream (page 186)

Halve the canary melon and
remove the seeds with a spoon.
Add 2–3 scoops of vanilla ice cream to
the middle of each melon half and
serve with a spoon.

WATERMELON SALAD
WITH FETA, TOMATO, MINT
AND CUCUMBER

On hot summer days, I can eat this salad constantly.
The sweet, juicy watermelon in combination with the fleshy
oxheart tomatoes could not go better with the crisp,
thickly sliced cucumbers and salty feta.

1 small seedless watermelon
1 Lebanese (short) cucumber
3–4 oxheart tomatoes
3–4 mint sprigs
200 g (7 oz) feta
fleur de sel, to taste
olive oil, for drizzling
juice of ½ lemon

Halve the watermelon, remove pieces of the flesh
using a spoon and arrange on a large plate. Peel
the cucumber and cut into thick slices. Cut the tomatoes
into chunks and arrange on the watermelon, along
with the cucumber. Pick the mint leaves and tear
into smaller pieces.

Crumble the feta over the salad, scatter over the mint
and fleur de sel, and drizzle with olive oil and
the lemon juice.

WATERMELON RIND CHUTNEY

This is a favourite recipe from my book Von der Schale bis zum Kern (From Skin to Seed), *which has already converted many sceptics. I like this chutney best with soft goat's cheese or a mature hard cheese and fresh scones (biscuits).*

1 kg (2 lb 3 oz) watermelon rind with pith
3 cm (1¼ in) piece ginger
½ red chilli
300 ml (10 fl oz) apple cider vinegar
300 g (10½ oz) sugar
1 strip lemon zest
4 whole allspice berries
1 teaspoon salt
1 cinnamon stick
1 teaspoon your favourite curry powder

Cut the green skin away from the rind of the melon. Slice the melon rind, along with the white part of the fruit into 2 cm (¾ in) pieces. Peel and finely chop the ginger. Finely chop the chilli with the seeds. Combine the melon, ginger and chilli with the remaining ingredients and 300 ml (10 fl oz) water in a large saucepan and bring to the boil. Reduce the heat and simmer for about 1 hour, until the watermelon rind is translucent.

Fill sterilised jars with the still-hot chutney, seal tightly and allow to cool. Refrigerate for 1 day before using, to allow the flavours to develop. The chutney will keep in the fridge for up to 3 months.

PICKLED
WATERMELON

*With a spoonful of yoghurt as a topping for hot curries or meat dishes,
or chopped with mint and olive oil on grilled lamb chops, pickled watermelon
is a constant companion that you will never tire of.*

1 small seedless watermelon (about 800 g/1 lb 12 oz)
1 lemon
600 ml (20½ fl oz) white wine vinegar
200 g (7 oz) sugar
3 peppercorns
1 bay leaf
½ teaspoon salt

Cut the watermelon, including the rind, into slices and then into 1 cm
(½ in) thick triangles. Place in a large saucepan. Peel thin strips of zest
from the lemon using a vegetable peeler and slice into thin lengths. In
a smaller saucepan, mix the lemon zest with the vinegar, 200 ml (7 fl oz)
water, the sugar, peppercorns, bay leaf and salt. Bring to the boil and
simmer for about 2 minutes, until the sugar dissolves. Pour the liquid over
the melon.

So that the melon pieces remain submerged in the liquid, cut a disc of
baking paper the diameter of the saucepan, lay on top of the melon and
weigh down with a plate. Simmer for about 45 minutes over low heat, or
until the white part of the melon is translucent, the pink flesh is almost
jelly-like and the green rind al dente*.

Remove the saucepan from the stovetop and allow the melon to cool a
little. Fill sterilised jars with the pickled melon, pour over the liquid and
keep in the fridge for up to 1 year.

---

* If the green rind is still hard, peel it away before serving.

P

PEACHES, PEARS, PLUMS

TEA-POACHED PEACHES
WITH SALTED YOGHURT
AND TARRAGON

I remember watching with excitement as my host mother in California poached and skinned peaches. As soon as I tasted the sweet fruit, I knew from then on I would always love peaches cooked this way.

4 peaches
2 teaspoons Earl Grey tea leaves
90 g (3 oz/¼ cup) honey
300 g (10½ oz) Greek-style yoghurt
scraped seeds of ½ vanilla bean
fleur de sel and freshly ground black pepper, to taste
2–3 tarragon sprigs

Score the underside of the peaches with a cross. Bring 300 ml (10 fl oz) water to the boil in a saucepan, then immerse the peaches in the water for 30 seconds. Remove and refresh in iced water, then remove the skin. Return the water to the boil, place the tea in a tea egg or infuser and infuse in the water for 3–5 minutes. Remove the infuser and add the honey to sweeten the tea. Remove from the heat and immerse the peaches in the tea and leave for at least 30 minutes, or overnight to absorb the flavour.

Flavour the yoghurt with the vanilla seeds and a pinch of fleur de sel. Divide the yoghurt among plates and sit the peaches on the yoghurt. Drizzle a little of the tea liquid over the peaches, and serve garnished with fleur de sel, pepper and tarragon.

GRILLED PEACH
WITH BACON AND RICOTTA
ON TOAST

---

*Toast or open sandwiches offer endless possibilities for
serving small dishes without cutlery. Because everything
tastes better when you eat it with your fingers!*

---

6 peaches
12 rashers (slices) bacon or prosciutto
1–2 sage sprigs, plus extra leaves to garnish
1 teaspoon olive oil
4 slices sourdough bread
2 tablespoons butter
150 g (5½ oz) ricotta
1–2 teaspoons honey
freshly ground black pepper, to taste

Preheat the oven to 180°C (350°F) (conventional) and
line a baking tray with baking paper. Halve the peaches,
remove the stones and wrap each half in a rasher of
bacon. Place the peaches on the prepared tray. Pick the
sage leaves and place on top of the peaches. Drizzle with
the olive oil and bake for 8–10 minutes.

Meanwhile, spread both sides of the bread with the
butter and toast on both sides in a chargrill pan. Allow
the bread to cool a little, then spread the ricotta on top.
Add the peach halves, then drizzle with honey and season
with pepper to serve.

PEACHES WITH BURRATA, MINT AND BREAD CHIPS

This dish is a sensual balance of different flavours and textures. While the runny centre of the burrata coats the sweet and sour peaches, the freshness of the mint and the strong flavour of the olives complete the composition. Add crisp bread chips, peppery olive oil and salt that crunches in the mouth – and you have the taste of pure happiness!

¼ sourdough baguette
1 burrata
2–3 poached peaches (see page 143)
1 tablespoon olives
1–2 mint sprigs
olive oil, for drizzling
coarse sea salt and freshly ground black pepper, to taste

Preheat the oven to 170°C (340°F) (conventional).
For the bread chips, very thinly slice the sourdough baguette and toast in the oven for 8–10 minutes, or until golden brown.

Rip the burrata cheese into pieces and divide among plates. Slice the peaches and place on top of the burrata. Using your fingers, break the olives into pieces, removing the pits as you go. Pick the mint leaves and scatter over the burrata and peaches, along with the torn olives. Drizzle with olive oil and crumble over the bread chips. To finish, season with coarse sea salt and pepper.

PEACH AND PISTACHIO GALETTE

This recipe has been a constant companion since my time at Chez Panisse, and you couldn't find a more simple, yet complex-tasting dish! Whether it's made with apples, apricots, peaches or damsons, it can be topped with whatever the heart desires. Instead of pistachios in the filling, almonds or chestnuts also taste great.

Base
250 g (9 oz) plain (all-purpose) flour,
plus extra for dusting
2 tablespoons caster (superfine) sugar
pinch of salt
150 g (5½ oz) cold butter
90 ml (3 fl oz) iced water

Filling
100 g (3½ oz) shelled pistachios
70 g (2½ oz) butter
scraped seeds of ½ vanilla bean
50 g (1¾ oz) caster (superfine) sugar

Topping
8 poached peaches (see page 143)
100 g (3½ oz) butter
15 g (½ oz) shelled pistachios
1 tablespoon caster (superfine) sugar,
for sprinkling

For the base, mix the flour, sugar and salt in a bowl. Cut the butter into small cubes. Using your fingertips, rub the butter into the flour, making sure there are still visible pieces of butter in the dough – this is the secret to a crisp base. Add the cold water and quickly form the dough into a rough ball. Don't knead – the butter pieces should remain visible and not melt. Flatten the dough slightly, wrap in plastic wrap and refrigerate for at least 30 minutes.

Meanwhile, for the filling, very finely grind the pistachios in a food processor. Melt the butter in a small saucepan over low heat. In a bowl, mix the ground pistachios, butter, vanilla seeds and sugar to form a paste.

Preheat the oven to 180°C (350°F) (conventional). For the topping, halve the peaches, remove the stones and very thinly slice the flesh. Melt the butter in a small saucepan over low heat.

On a lightly floured work surface, roll the pastry out to a 3 mm (⅛ in) thick circle. Place on a baking sheet lined with baking paper and spread the pistachio filling over the pastry, leaving a 2–3 cm (¾–1¼ in) border. Arrange the peach slices on top like roof tiles, or however you like. Fold up the edge of the pastry, then brush the peach liberally and the pastry edges only lightly with the melted butter. Roughly chop the pistachios and scatter around the edge. Sprinkle the sugar over the top.

Bake the galette for 30–40 minutes, or until golden brown. Rotate the baking sheet once or twice, to ensure that the galette is evenly baked.

PEACH CHUTNEY
WITH ALMONDS

Whether served as a sweet and sour accompaniment to curries or grilled lamb, in a sandwich or with cream cheese, chutneys make a lovely addition to many dishes.

125 ml (4 fl oz / ½ cup) apple cider vinegar
180 g (6½ oz) sugar
200 g (7 oz) blanched almonds
½ yellow capsicum (bell pepper)
1 small white onion
1 red chilli

1 cardamom pod
1 garlic clove
2 cm (¾ in) piece ginger
50 g (1¾ oz) sultanas (golden raisins)
½ teaspoon salt
1 kg (2 lb 3 oz) peaches

Combine the vinegar and sugar in a large saucepan, bring to the boil and simmer until the sugar dissolves. Toast the almonds in a dry frying pan for a few minutes until golden. Remove the seeds and membranes from the capsicum, then dice the flesh. Peel and dice the onion. Halve the chilli lengthways, remove the seeds and finely chop. Press lightly on the cardamom pod with the back of a knife. Peel and thinly slice the garlic. Peel and finely grate the ginger.

Add all the ingredients except the peaches to the vinegar and sugar mixture, and simmer over low heat for 10 minutes. Meanwhile, halve the peaches, remove the stones and roughly chop. Add the peach to the pan and simmer for a further 10–15 minutes. Fill sterilised jars with the still-hot chutney and seal the jars immediately. Allow to cool, then refrigerate for 1 day for the flavours to develop.

The chutney will keep in the fridge for up to 3 months.

PEACH AND ALMOND CAKE
WITH HONEY CARAMEL

*This beautifully moist flourless cake can also be made with pears, apricots,
apples or quinces.*

4–5 poached peaches (page 143)
1 tablespoon butter, plus extra
for greasing
4 eggs
100 g (3½ oz) caster (superfine) sugar
200 g (7 oz) ground almonds
1½ teaspoons baking powder

200 g (7 oz) ricotta
1 tablespoon cornflour (cornstarch)
100 g (3½ oz) honey
250 g (9 oz) thickened (whipping)
cream

Preheat the oven to 170°C (340°F) (conventional). Grease and line a round
cake tin with baking paper. Cut the poached peaches in half, remove the
stones and cut into wedges. Melt the butter in a frying pan and cook the
peach wedges until lightly caramelised.

In a large bowl, beat the eggs and sugar until well combined. In a separate
bowl, combine the ground almonds with the baking powder, then stir into the
beaten egg, along with the ricotta and cornflour. Spread half the cake batter
into the prepared tin, then scatter the peach wedges on top. Cover with the
remaining batter, then bake for 35 minutes in the middle of the oven. Reduce
the temperature to 150°C (300°F) and bake for a further 15 minutes, or until
a skewer inserted into the cake comes out clean.

Allow the cake to cool, then remove it from the tin.
In a small pan, warm the honey and cream together until the mixture
reduces by half and resembles a caramel. Allow to cool, then whisk the honey
caramel until smooth and glossy. Serve with the cake.

PEAR AND CELERIAC 'CAPPUCCINO' WITH COCOA AND FRUIT BREAD

The sweetness of celeriac and pears goes really well with the bitter taste of cocoa.

Cappuccino
1 tablespoon butter
1 tablespoon olive oil
2 French shallots
1 garlic clove
1 small celeriac bulb
2 firm pears
2–3 cm (¾–1¼ in) piece ginger
1 bay leaf
2 thyme sprigs
1 teaspoon fennel seeds
1 teaspoon finely grated lemon zest
4 teaspoons dry white wine

500 ml (17 fl oz/2 cups) vegetable stock
200 ml (7 fl oz) coconut milk
salt and freshly ground black pepper, to taste

Fruit bread
300 g (10½ oz) spelt flour
60 g (2 oz) rye flour
2 teaspoons baking powder
2 teaspoons gingerbread spices (available from specialist stores)
pinch of salt

60 g (2 oz) butter
340 g (12 oz) honey
1 teaspoon finely grated orange zest
200 g (7 oz) cooked sweet chestnuts
300 g (10½ oz) mixed nuts (e.g. walnuts, almonds, pine nuts)
400 g (14 oz) dried fruit (e.g. raisins, dates, prunes, cranberries)
6–8 sage leaves
milk, for foaming
cocoa powder, for dusting

For the cappuccino, melt the butter with the olive oil in a saucepan. Peel and finely dice the shallots and garlic, then add to the pan and sauté for about 5 minutes over low heat. Peel the celeriac. Peel and core the pears, then cut both the celeriac and pear into rough pieces. Peel and finely chop or grate the ginger, then add to the saucepan, along with the bay leaf, thyme, fennel seeds, lemon zest, pear and celeriac. Add the wine and allow to reduce for a few minutes. Pour in the stock and coconut milk, and simmer for 20 minutes. Remove the bay leaf and thyme sprigs, purée the soup and season with salt and pepper.

For the fruit bread, preheat the oven to 190°C (375°F) (conventional). Line a loaf (bar) tin with baking paper. Combine the flours, baking powder, gingerbread spices

and salt in a bowl. Melt the butter with the honey in a small saucepan over medium heat. Add the orange zest and 240 ml (8 fl oz) water, then remove from the heat. Add the honey and butter mixture to the flour mixture and carefully fold in. Roughly chop the nuts and dried fruit and stir into the dough.

Fill the prepared tin with the dough, lay the sage leaves on top and bake for about 1 hour, until a skewer inserted into the bread comes out clean. If the top of the bread becomes too dark, cover it with foil.

To serve, reheat the cappucino soup and share among bowls or mugs. Foam up the milk in a small saucepan, then add 1 tablespoon to each bowl and sprinkle with cocoa powder. Serve with the fruit bread on the side.

GRANOLA WITH YOGHURT
AND SAFFRON PEARS

*People who know me know I can't begin the day without muesli. I always serve
it cold or warm with fruit, yoghurt and honey, It is especially delicious with saffron pears.*

Saffron pears
4 small pears
500 ml (17 fl oz/2 cups) pear juice
pinch of saffron threads
1 cinnamon stick
2 cardamom pods, lightly bruised
½ vanilla bean
1 slice ginger

Granola
150 g (5½ oz) honey, plus extra to serve
300 g (10½ oz) mixed nuts (e.g. hazelnuts, almonds,
walnuts, cashew nuts)
450 g (1 lb) rolled (porridge) oats, einkorn wheat, spelt,
rye, buckwheat or farro, or a mix

80 g (2¾ oz) golden linseeds (flax seeds)
80 g (2¾ oz) sunflower seeds
50 g (1¾ oz) pepitas (pumpkin seeds)
2 tablespoons sesame seeds
1 teaspoon finely grated orange zest
juice of 1 orange
1 teaspoon finely grated lemon zest
scraped seeds of ½ vanilla bean
¼ teaspoon salt
140 ml (5 fl oz) olive oil
100 g (3½ oz) dried fruit (e.g. raisins, dates, prunes,
apricots, cherries)
50 g (1¾ oz) shelled pistachios

To serve
500 g (1 lb 2 oz) Greek-style yoghurt

For the saffron pears, peel the pears and pour the pear
juice into a saucepan. Bring to the boil, along with
the spices, vanilla bean and ginger, then add the pears
and boil for 2–3 minutes. Remove from the heat and
leave the pears to infuse in the hot juice.

For the granola, preheat the oven to 170°C (340°F)
(conventional). Gently heat the honey in a small
saucepan. Roughly chop the larger nuts. In a bowl,
thoroughly mix all the granola ingredients except the
dried fruit and pistachios. Pour over the warmed honey
and, using your hands, mix together well, pushing some

of the mixture into larger clumps. Spread the granola
over two or three baking trays lined with baking paper.
Toast in the oven for 25–30 minutes, stirring every
10–15 minutes, until golden brown.

Let the granola cool, then stir through your preferred
dried fruit (chopping up the larger pieces) and the
pistachios. Store in a jar with an airtight lid. The
granola will keep for about 3 months.

Serve the granola with the yoghurt, saffron pears
and extra honey.

PORK CUTLETS
WITH CARAMELISED PEARS
AND SAGE

*Roast and caramel flavours combine here with smoky wooden-barrel notes
of Cognac and creamy, sour crème fraîche.*

4 pork cutlets
salt and freshly ground black pepper
1 bunch sage
2 tablespoons clarified butter
4 small pears
6 French shallots
1 garlic clove
5 juniper berries
5 peppercorns
1 bay leaf
40 ml (1¼ fl oz) Cognac
100 g (3½ oz) crème fraîche

Preheat the oven to 120°C (250°F) (conventional). Season the cutlets
with salt and pepper. Pick the sage leaves. Heat half the clarified butter
in a frying pan over high heat. Add the sage leaves and cutlets, and
quickly sear the meat on both sides. Transfer the cutlets and sage to an
ovenproof dish and cook in the oven for 15 minutes.

Halve or quarters the pears. Peel and halve the shallots, and bruise the
garlic clove. Heat the remaining clarified butter in the same pan and cook
the pear, shallot and garlic until golden brown. Add the juniper berries,
peppercorns, bay leaf and cognac, and very carefully set alight to burn off
the alcohol. Stir in the crème fraîche. Remove the cutlets from the oven
and transfer them to the sauce. Spoon the sauce over the cutlets for the
flavours to combine, then season with salt and pepper and serve.

This goes well with creamy polenta or fresh white bread.

GINGER AND PEAR CAKE
WITH COFFEE CREAM

I first tried this cake at a staff dinner at Chez Panisse. Every time I eat it I'm taken straight back to Alice Waters' kitchen. I've studded this dark, moist ginger and molasses cake with pears, to lend it a certain freshness.

Coffee cream
100 g (3½ oz) coffee beans
1 tablespoon icing (confectioners') sugar
200 ml (7 fl oz) thickened (whipping) cream

Cake
150 g (5½ oz) caster (superfine) sugar
300 g (10½ oz) molasses or golden syrup

200 ml (7 fl oz) peanut oil
2 eggs
60 g (2 oz) fresh ginger
180 ml (6½ fl oz) hot water
2 teaspoons baking powder
340 g (12 oz) plain (all-purpose) flour
½ teaspoon ground cinnamon
1 teaspoon finely grated orange zest
3–5 small pears

For the coffee cream, mix all the ingredients together and refrigerate for at least 3 hours or overnight for the flavours to infuse.

Preheat the oven to 180°C (350°F) (conventional). For the cake, combine the sugar, molasses and peanut oil in a large bowl. Lightly beat the eggs and stir into the sugar and oil mixture. Peel the ginger and finely grate or very finely chop. In a small bowl, mix the hot water with the baking powder. Sift the flour and cinnamon into another bowl. Stir in all the cake ingredients except the pears and leave to rest for 10 minutes.

Line a large loaf (bar) tin with baking paper. Add the cake mixture and insert the whole pears. Bake for 1–1½ hours, until a skewer inserted into the cake comes out clean. Allow the cake to cool, then remove from the tin.

Strain the cream, whip until thick and serve with the cake.

YEASTED PLUM CAKE

This classic Austrian yeasted dough cake with streusel reminds me of late summer days spent playing in the garden.

Dough
250 ml (8½ fl oz/1 cup) milk
21 g (¾ oz) fresh or dried yeast
70 g (2½ oz) caster (superfine) sugar
500 g (1 lb 2 oz) plain (all-purpose) flour,
plus extra for dusting
80 g (2¾ oz) butter
pinch of salt
grated zest of ½ lemon
1 egg
1 egg yolk

Topping
1½ kg (3 lb 5 oz) plums

Streusel
140 g (5 oz) butter
80 g (2¾ oz) caster (superfine) sugar
70 g (2½ oz) plain (all-purpose) flour
70 g (2½ oz) ground hazelnuts
½ teaspoon cinnamon
pinch of salt
scraped seeds of ½ vanilla bean

Warm the milk in a small saucepan over low heat. In a large bowl, combine the yeast, 1 teaspoon of the sugar and 150 g (5½ oz/1 cup) of the flour. Pour in the milk and briefly combine. Set aside in a warm place for 20 minutes.

Melt the butter. Place the remaining flour and sugar in the bowl of a stand mixer with a dough hook. Add the yeast mixture, salt, lemon zest, eggs and melted butter, then knead for about 5 minutes, until you have a smooth dough. Cover, and set aside in a warm place for 40–50 minutes.

Meanwhile, quarter the plums and remove the stones.

For the streusel, place all the ingredients in a large bowl and rub together using your fingertips, until the mixture resembles a crumble.

Preheat the oven to 200°C (400°F) (conventional). Line a baking tray with baking paper. On a lightly floured work surface, knead the dough for a few minutes, then roll the dough out to the same size as the baking tray. Carefully transfer the dough to the baking tray, scatter over the plums and sprinkle with the streusel. Cover, and set aside for a further 15 minutes.

Bake for 45–50 minutes, until a skewer inserted into the cake comes out clean and the plums are caramelised and golden brown.

PULLED DUCK BURGER
WITH PLUM SAUCE

Between two slices of bread, pulled duck becomes a stylish and delicious gourmet fast food.
This dish is best enjoyed in the evening with friends. Place everything in the middle of the table,
so people can assemble their own burgers.

Serves 6

Slow-cooked duck
1 organic duck (about 2.5 kg/5½ lb),
gutted and cleaned
salt and freshly ground black pepper

Plum sauce
1 small red onion
2 garlic cloves
1 cm (½ in) piece ginger
1 tablespoon olive oil
4 mirabelle or other small yellow
plums
1 small red capsicum (bell pepper)
60 ml (2 fl oz/¼ cup) soy sauce
2 teaspoons honey
1 teaspoon rice or white-wine vinegar
2 teaspoons ajvar
pinch of pimentón
salt and freshly ground black pepper,
to taste

Burger rolls
125 g (4½ oz) butter
200 ml (7 fl oz) milk
400 g (14 oz) plain (all-purpose)
flour, plus extra for dusting
21 g (¾ oz) fresh or dried yeast
1 teaspoon honey
1 teaspoon salt
1 egg
yoghurt, for spreading
sesame seeds or gomashio,
for sprinkling

Coleslaw
2–3 carrots
1 apple
½ head red cabbage
½ head white cabbage
1 small fennel bulb
3–4 radishes
1 small bunch parsley
juice of 1 lemon
juice of 1 orange

1 teaspoon honey
3 tablespoons white-wine vinegar
3 tablespoons olive oil
2 tablespoons dijon mustard
250 g (9 oz) yoghurt
1 teaspoon mustard seeds
salt and freshly ground black pepper,
to taste

To assemble
1 small red onion
⅛ head red cabbage
3 plums
90 g (3 oz/⅓ cup) mustard

Preheat the oven to 190°C (375°F) (conventional). Wash the duck, pat dry with paper towel and season with salt and pepper. Lay the duck in a roasting tin and roast for 15–20 minutes, then reduce the oven temperature to 150°C (300°F) and cook for a further 3 hours. Turn every 30 minutes.

Remove the duck from the oven, allow to cool a little and, pulling with two forks, tear the meat into strips lengthways. Reserve the duck fat from the tin.

For the plum sauce, peel the onion, garlic and ginger and finely chop. Heat the oil in a frying pan and sauté the chopped ingredients for 5 minutes. Remove the stones from the plums and cut into wedges. Remove the seeds and membrane from the capsicum and roughly dice. Add the plum and capsicum to the pan, along with the remaining plum sauce ingredients and simmer over low heat for 20 minutes. Mix the meat with the sauce and a little of the reserved duck fat.

For the burger rolls, melt the butter in a small saucepan, then remove from the heat and stir in the milk. Place the flour in a bowl and make a well in the middle. Crumble the yeast into the well, then add the honey and 100 ml (3½ fl oz) of the butter and milk mixture. Stir the yeast and milk mixture together, working in a little flour from the edge of the well. Cover with a little of the flour from the bowl, then cover with a clean tea towel (dish towel) and leave to rest for 15 minutes.

Add the remaining butter and milk mixture, along with the salt and egg, then knead for about 5 minutes, until you have a smooth dough. Cover again with the towel and leave to rise for 40 minutes.

Preheat the oven to 190°C (375°F) (conventional). Briefly knead the dough on a lightly floured work surface, then divide into six pieces. Form each piece into a ball and place them on a baking tray lined with baking paper. Using a pastry brush, coat each bun in a thin layer of yoghurt, scatter over the sesame seeds or gomashio and leave uncovered for 15 minutes. Bake for 20–25 minutes, until golden.

For the coleslaw, peel the carrots and core the apple. Coarsely grate the vegetables and the apple. Finely chop the parsley. Combine all the coleslaw ingredients in a bowl and mix well. Season with salt and pepper and leave for 20 minutes for the flavours to develop.

Peel the onion and thinly shave using a mandoline. Shave the cabbage just as thinly, and thinly slice the plums. To serve, halve the burger rolls and spread a little duck fat and mustard on the cut sides. Top with the pulled duck, plum, onion, red cabbage and burger tops, and serve with the coleslaw on the side. Alternatively, you can mix the fresh plums into the coleslaw rather than putting them directly on the burger.

ROAST CHICKEN
WITH GREENGAGES

Greengages are yellow–green to orange–red stone fruit that belong to the plum family, and they are often found growing in old orchards or Grandma's garden. The combination of this little fruit with chicken, lemons and spices is simply unbeatable. I know of no other oven-cooked meal that so beautifully balances sweet and sour flavours. If you can't find greengages, simply use mirabelle plums or grapes.

1 organic chicken, broken into pieces by your butcher
1 tablespoon olive oil
1 teaspoon your favourite curry powder
1 teaspoon salt
4 garlic cloves, unpeeled
1 lemon
2 cm (¾ in) piece ginger
250 g (9 oz) greengages

4–6 fresh or 6–7 dried bay leaves
3 thyme sprigs
1 tablespoon soy sauce
1 tablespoon maple syrup
coarse sea salt and freshly ground black pepper, to taste

To serve
fresh baguette or cooked rice

Preheat the oven to 200°C (400°F) (conventional). Wash the chicken pieces and pat dry with paper towel, then place in a roasting tin. Rub the olive oil, curry and salt into the chicken and leave to marinate for 10 minutes. Lightly bruise the garlic cloves and add to the roasting tin. Halve the lemon lengthways, then thinly slice and add to the tin. Give everything a good mix, then roast for 30 minutes, turning frequently.

Peel and finely grate the ginger, then place around the chicken with the greengages, bay leaves and thyme. Pour over the soy sauce and maple syrup, give everything a stir, then roast for a further 15 minutes.

Remove the chicken from the oven and season with salt and pepper. Serve with a fresh baguette or rice.

PLUM AND FENNEL SALAD
WITH GINGER DRESSING AND SESAME SEEDS

*This extra-quick salad is also excellent made with celery
or cucumber instead of fennel.*

juice of ½ orange
1 tablespoon white-wine vinegar
1 teaspoon honey
60 ml (2 fl oz/¼ cup) olive oil, plus extra for drizzling
pinch of salt
1 cm (½ in) piece ginger
3 plums
1 small fennel bulb
1 tablespoon toasted sesame seeds

Combine the orange juice, vinegar, honey, oil and salt
in a screw-top jar. Peel and finely grate the ginger,
and add to the jar, then seal and shake well. Using a
mandoline, thinly shave the plums and fennel (setting
the fronds aside). Transfer to a bowl and toss well
with the dressing. Marinate for 20 minutes.

Drizzle the salad with extra olive oil, scatter over the
sesame seeds and garnish with the reserved
fennel fronds.

DAMSON OR
PLUM JAM

Good things take time.

---

2 kg (4 lb 6 oz) very ripe damsons or other plums
3 tablespoons sugar
1 cinnamon stick
4 teaspoons rum

Halve the damsons or plums and remove the stones.
Slowly caramelise the sugar in a large saucepan, then
add the fruit and cinnamon stick and stir well. Loosen
with the rum. Bring to the boil, stirring constantly,
then reduce the heat to the lowest setting and simmer,
stirring frequently, for 6–7 hours, until reduced.
Fill sterilised jars with the still-hot damson or plum
jam and seal immediately.

The jam will keep in the fridge for up to 1 year.

SWEET–SOUR PICKLED
MIRABELLE PLUMS

---

*I love eating Arctic char or trout cooked at low
temperature with a few pickled mirabelle plums.
They lend the fish a pleasant sourness and help
it stay moist.*

---

1 kg (2 lb 3 oz) mirabelle plums
500 ml (17 fl oz/2 cups) fruit vinegar
300 g (10½ oz) sugar
1 star anise
½ teaspoon salt
1 strip lemon zest
3–4 bay leaves
2–3 thyme sprigs
1 slice ginger
1 teaspoon mustard seeds
1 teaspoon coriander seeds

Score the plums with a cross at the top and bottom
or prick a few times with a skewer. In a saucepan,
combine the remaining ingredients with 500 ml
(17 fl oz/2 cups) water and bring to the boil. Simmer
until the sugar dissolves. Add the plums and gently
simmer for a further 5–8 minutes. Remove the
plums with a skimmer or slotted spoon, then transfer
to sterilised jars. Bring the vinegar mixture to the
boil again then pour over the plums. Seal the jars
immediately.

The pickled plums will keep in the fridge for about
1 year.

DAMSON
BUNS

These buns will always remind me of afternoon coffee with my grandma.
Sweet yeast dough – whether she made it for buchteln rolls, reindling cake
or rohrnudeln buns – was her specialty.

---

260 ml (9 fl oz) lukewarm milk
500 g (1 lb 2 oz) plain (all-purpose) flour
2 tablespoons honey
2 tablespoons caster (superfine) sugar
25 g (1 oz) fresh yeast
180 g (6½ oz) butter, plus extra
for greasing
scraped seeds of ½ vanilla bean
½ teaspoon salt

2 eggs
1 egg yolk
4 teaspoons rum
finely grated zest of 1 lemon
or orange
15–20 damsons (depending on size)
about 100 g/3½ oz) Plum jam (jelly)
(page 167)
icing (confectioners') sugar, for dusting

In a bowl, combine 100 ml (3½ fl oz) of the milk, 30 g (1 oz) of the flour, and
the honey, sugar and yeast to make a loose dough. Cover and leave for about
20 minutes to rise. Melt 150 g (5½ oz) of the butter and allow to cool a little. Add
the butter, vanilla seeds, salt, eggs, rum and lemon or orange zest to the dough,
and knead until smooth. Form the dough into a ball, then cover and leave in a
warm place until doubled in size.

Meanwhile, halve the damsons without cutting all the way through, remove the
stones and replace with ½ teaspoon plum jam per damson.

Preheat the oven to 180°C (350°F) (conventional). Divide the dough into
15–20 small balls, then flatten slightly. Place one damson on top of each disc,
then carefully seal the dough around the fruit and roll back into balls. Melt the
remaining butter, then roll the dough balls in the butter to coat well. Arrange the
dough balls close together, seam side down, in a round cake tin greased with butter.
Cover and leave to rise for another 30 minutes.

Brush the buns with the left-over melted butter and bake for
30–40 minutes. Leave to cool, dust liberally with icing sugar and enjoy.

PLUM
UPSIDE-DOWN CAKE

Almonds, yoghurt and olive oil give this cake its moistness, but sunflower oil or mild canola oil also work just as well. If you like it a bit more intense, mix in a few spoonfuls of almond oil.

butter, for greasing
6 plums
finely grated zest of 1 lemon
5 eggs
150 g (5½ oz) caster (superfine) sugar
150 g (5½ oz) blossom honey
scraped seeds of ½ vanilla bean

pinch of salt
200 ml (7 fl oz) olive oil
100 g (3½ oz) yoghurt
150 g (5½ oz) semolina
150 g (5½ oz) ground almonds
2 teaspoons baking powder
whipped cream, to serve

Preheat the oven to 190°C (375°F) (conventional). Lightly grease a round 25 cm (10 in) cake tin with butter and line with baking paper.

Remove the stones from the plums, cut into wedges and arrange, cut side down, over the bottom of the tin. In a food processor, combine the lemon zest, eggs, sugar, honey, vanilla seeds and salt for 5 minutes until foamy. Still processing, pour in the olive oil in a thin stream, then process for a further 3 minutes. Finally, mix in the yoghurt. Transfer to a large bowl. In another bowl, combine the semolina, ground almonds and baking powder, then carefully fold into the egg mixture.

Spread the batter evenly over the plums, then bake for about 1 hour, or until a skewer inserted into the cake comes out clean. Allow the cake to cool a little, then remove from the tin and serve with whipped cream.

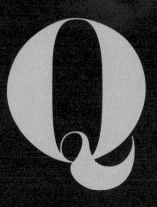

QUINCES

QUINCE TARTE TATIN

I especially like the balance between sweet and sour in this tarte tatin.
Quinces develop an almost creamy consistency during baking and literally melt in the mouth.
This tart is best enjoyed lukewarm with a spoonful of crème fraîche or vanilla ice cream.

Poached quinces	*Pastry*	*Caramel*
100 g (3½ oz) sugar	250 g (9 oz) plain (all-purpose) flour	100 g (3½ oz) caster (superfine) sugar
1 star anise	2 tablespoons caster (superfine) sugar	20 g (¾ oz) cold butter
½ vanilla bean	pinch of salt	
2–3 lemon slices	150 g (5½ oz) cold butter, plus	
4–5 small quinces	1 tablespoon extra for greasing	
	90 ml (3 fl oz) iced water	

For the poached quinces, combine 1 litre (34 fl oz/4 cups) water, the sugar, star anise, vanilla bean and lemon slices in a saucepan. Wash the quinces thoroughly, rub off the downy fur, then peel and halve or cut into quarters. Immediately place the quince in the liquid, to prevent it going brown. Cook over low heat until the quince is soft. Remove from the heat and leave to cool. Carefully remove the cores using a sharp knife.

For the pastry, mix the flour, sugar and salt in a bowl. Cut the butter into small cubes. Using your fingertips, rub the butter into the flour mixture, making sure there are still visible pieces of butter in the dough. Add the water and quickly shape the dough into a ball. Press the pastry into a flat dish, then wrap in plastic wrap and refrigerate for at least 30 minutes.

Preheat the oven to 200°C (400°F) (conventional). Grease a flan (tart) tin with the extra butter. For the caramel, melt the sugar in a small frying pan over low heat until golden brown. Immediately stir in the butter. Spread the caramel in the tin and arrange the quince, round side down and tightly packed, on top.

Remove the pastry from the fridge and, using a rolling pin, roll out into a disc 2–3 cm (¾–1¼ in) larger than the tin and 3 mm (⅛ in) thick. Lay the pastry over the quince and push the edges into the tin. Bake the tart for 30–35 minutes, until golden brown.

Remove the tart from the oven and allow to cool a little. Lay a large plate upside down on top of the tin and, using oven gloves to assist you, quickly but carefully turn the tart over (don't let the hot caramel run out!). Lift the tin off the tart and serve while still warm.

The poaching liquid can be used to sweeten muesli, yoghurt or cakes. Or add it to cocktails!

WILD BOAR RAGOUT
WITH QUINCE

*I admit that it was a long time before I dared to use quinces in my recipes.
Only during my time at Babette's did I teach myself how wonderful quinces taste
in a game or lamb stew, and just how versatile they are in general.*

1 onion
2 garlic cloves
300 g (10½ oz) root vegetables of your choice
800 g (1 lb 12 oz) wild boar shoulder
salt
3–4 tablespoons olive oil
1 slice ginger
2 tablespoons tomato paste (concentrated purée)
2 tablespoons game spice mix (available
from specialist stores)
1 cinnamon stick
2 thyme sprigs
2 rosemary sprigs

750 ml (25½ fl oz/3 cups) red wine
500 ml (17 fl oz/2 cups) game or beef stock
2 quinces
1 small red kuri pumpkin (winter squash)
2 tablespoons Elderberry jam (jelly) (page 93)
finely grated zest of 1 orange
1 piece bitter dark chocolate
salt and freshly ground black pepper, to taste

To serve
creamy polenta, couscous, mashed potato
or sourdough bread

Preheat the oven to 150°C (300°F) (conventional). Peel and finely dice the onion and garlic. Coarsely grate the root vegetables. Cut the meat into 4 × 4 cm (1½ × 1½ in) cubes. Heat a flameproof casserole dish on the stovetop and add the olive oil. Working in batches, sear the meat quickly over high heat until brown, then season well with salt. Transfer the meat to a plate. Fry the onion, garlic and ginger over high heat. Add the tomato paste and brown quickly, then add the spices and herbs and return the meat to the pan.

Pour in the wine and stock. Bring briefly to the boil, then transfer to the lowest shelf of the oven for 2½ hours, until the meat is tender and juicy.

After 2 hours of cooking, thoroughly wash the quinces, rub off the downy fur, then peel, core and cut into quarters. Halve the pumpkin, remove the seeds and slice into wedges. Add the quince, pumpkin, elderberry jam, orange zest and chocolate to the ragout in the last 25–30 minutes of cooking and cook until the quince is soft. Season with salt and pepper.

Serve with creamy polenta, couscous, mashed potato or sourdough bread.

QUINCE
NEGRONI

*This drink always makes me think of
sentimental films set in the countryside,
wild romance and autumn menus.*

ice cubes
200 ml (7 fl oz) quince poaching
liquid (see right)
40 ml (1¼ fl oz) gin
40 ml (1¼ fl oz) vermouth
40 ml (1¼ fl oz) campari
1 poached quince (see right), to garnish

Put ice cubes in two glasses, then divide the quince
poaching liquid, gin, vermouth and campari between
the glasses and stir briefly. Slice the poached quince
into wedges and use to garnish the drinks.

POACHED
QUINCE

*Poached quinces go with so many things: yoghurt and
granola, cream-topped chocolate cakes, game stew or
a salad of chestnuts, red cabbage and bacon.
And, naturally, with a cheese plate.*

1 lemon
1 litre (34 fl oz/4 cups) apple or pear juice
3–4 quinces
1 vanilla bean
2 cardamom pods
1 cinnamon stick
2–3 bay leaves

Thinly slice the lemon and place in a saucepan
with the apple or pear juice. Thoroughly wash the
quinces, rub off the downy fur, then peel and halve
and immediately immerse in the juice, so they don't
turn brown.

Split the vanilla bean lengthways and add to the
pan. Lightly press on the cardamom pods with the
back of a knife and add to the quince, along with
the cinnamon stick and bay leaves. Bring to the boil
then simmer over low heat for 10–15 minutes, until
the quince is soft. Leave the quince immersed in the
poaching liquid until cool. Remove the cores.

The poached quince will keep in the fridge,
well immersed in the juice, for up to 1 month.

The poaching liquid can be used to sweeten muesli,
yoghurt, cakes or drinks (see left).

QUINCE
CHUTNEY

Quince chutney is a sweet and sour preserve that works perfectly with strong-flavoured and spicy dishes, such as cheese, curries and fish. There should always be chutney in the pantry!

1.5 kg (3 lb 5 oz) quinces
2 French shallots
3 garlic cloves
1 cm (½ in) piece ginger
1 red chilli
1 tablespoon olive oil
1 teaspoon each yellow and brown mustard seeds
½ teaspoon coriander seeds
1 cinnamon stick
2 bay leaves
½ teaspoon each salt and black peppercorns
200 ml (7 fl oz) apple cider vinegar
200 g (7 oz) sugar
80 g (2¾ oz) sultanas (golden raisins)

Wash the quinces, rub off the downy fur, then peel, cut into quarters and carefully remove the cores. Cut the quince into wedges and then into cubes. Peel and finely dice the shallots, garlic and ginger. Halve the chilli, remove the seeds, and finely chop. Heat the olive oil in a frying pan and sauté the shallot, garlic and ginger, then add the chilli, mustard seeds, coriander seeds, cinnamon stick, bay leaves and salt and pepper, and fry, stirring, for 2–3 minutes. Add the quince and the remaining ingredients to the pan and simmer for 30–40 minutes, stirring frequently.

Fill sterilised jars with the still-hot chutney. It will keep in a cool, dark place for several months.

QUINCE
JAM

… or an Indian summer in a jar.

1.5 kg (3 lb 5 oz) quinces
juice of 2 lemons
2–3 oranges
300 g (10½ oz) jam (jelly) sugar (3:1 fruit to sugar)

Thoroughly wash the quinces and rub off the downy fur. Mix the lemon juice with 2 litres (68 fl oz/8 cups) water. Cut the quinces into large pieces and remove the cores. Immediately immerse in the lemon water, so they don't turn brown.

Place the quince pieces in a saucepan. Add 500 ml (17 fl oz/2 cups) of the lemon water and bring to the boil, then cover and simmer for 30–40 minutes over low heat until soft.

Line a sieve with muslin (cheesecloth) and sit over a small saucepan. Pour in the poached quince and liquid and leave to strain overnight. (Keep the quince pieces for other dishes, such as serving with fruit bread or spooned over yoghurt).

Squeeze enough orange juice into the quince juice to bring it up to 900 ml (30½ fl oz). Add the jam sugar, then stir and boil vigorously for 3 minutes. Immediately fill sterilised jars with the liquid and seal tightly.

The jam will keep in the fridge for up to 1 year.

QUINCE PASTE
(MEMBRILLO)

It's definitely worth making membrillo in large quantities, because it not only rounds off a cheese plate, but also goes perfectly with ham or bacon and can even be enjoyed as a sweet.

2 kg (4 lb 6 oz) quinces
2 kg (4 lb 6 oz) sugar

Thoroughly wash the quinces, rub off the downy fur, then peel, core and cut into wedges. Place in a large saucepan and add enough water to just cover. Bring to the boil, then simmer for 15–20 minutes, until the quince is soft. Remove from the heat and purée with a hand-held blender, then add the sugar. Return the purée to the heat and, stirring constantly and watching carefully as the quince purée can spit, cook until thickened and the bottom of the pan is visible each time you stir.

Line a loaf (bar) tin with baking paper, then fill with the quince purée. Leave in a dry place until completely cool and dried out. Cut the quince paste into cubes or diamonds.

The quince paste will keep in the fridge for about 1 year.

Cut into pieces and coated in sugar, it turns into sweets. For a delicious and simple tapas, top a slice of toasted ciabatta with a slice of manchego and quince paste, and drizzle with olive oil.

SUMMER SALAD BAGUETTE WITH RASPBERRIES, BAKED RICOTTA AND TEA EGGS

Raspberries and cream cheese have always gone well together. Soft goat's cheese or shaved pecorino are just as good in this dish, as are strawberries, peaches or melons.

Tea eggs	Baked ricotta	Baguette	Dressing
2 teaspoons ground coffee	2 thyme sprigs	1 sourdough baguette	100 ml (3½ fl oz) olive oil
2 tablespoons soy sauce	20 g (¾ oz) parmesan	1–2 tablespoons butter	juice of 1 lemon
2 black tea bags	250 g (9 oz) ricotta	3–4 radishes	1 teaspoon dijon mustard
1 cinnamon stick	2 tablespoons olive oil	1–2 small Lebanese (short)	1 teaspoon honey
4 cloves	1 teaspoon finely grated	cucumbers	2 tablespoons Raspberry
2 star anise	lemon zest	100 g (3½ oz) mixed salad	vinegar (page 192)
1 strip orange zest	½ teaspoon salt	leaves	salt and freshly ground black
4 eggs	freshly ground black pepper,	125 g (4½ oz/1 cup)	pepper, to taste
	to taste	raspberries	
		30 g (1 oz/1 cup) watercress	

For the eggs, combine the coffee, soy sauce, tea, spices and orange zest in a large bowl and pour over 500 ml (17 fl oz/2 cups) boiling water. Boil the eggs in a small saucepan for 6 minutes, then rinse in cold water. Tap all over with a spoon, then immerse the eggs in their shells in the marinade and refrigerate overnight.

Preheat the oven to 200°C (400°F) (conventional). For the baked ricotta, pick the thyme leaves and finely chop. Finely grate the parmesan. Place the thyme leaves and parmesan in a bowl and add the remaining baked ricotta ingredients. Mix well, then press into a small ovenproof dish and bake for 20–30 minutes.

Halve the baguette lengthways and spread each half with butter. Finely shave the radishes using a mandoline. Peel the cucumbers and thinly slice. Drape the salad leaves, radish and cucumber over the baguette. Chop the baked ricotta into pieces and arrange on top of the salad with the raspberries and watercress.

For the dressing, combine all the ingredients in a screw-top jar, then seal and shake well. Season with salt and pepper, to taste. Peel and halve the eggs. Drizzle the dressing over the baguette, then cut into portions and serve with the eggs.

HOT LOVE

'Hot love' is a classic local dish that's often seen on summer ice-cream menus, and it remains an eternal favourite from my childhood. Whenever I eat it, I am reminded of the smell of fresh, rustling summer hay.

Vanilla ice cream
1 vanilla bean
250 ml (8½ fl oz/1 cup) milk
150 g (5½ oz) sugar
6 egg yolks
pinch of salt
500 ml (17 fl oz/2 cups) thickened (whipping) cream

Waffle rolls
60 g (2 oz) egg white (about 2)
pinch of salt
40 g (1½ oz) icing (confectioners') sugar
15 g (½ oz) caster (superfine) sugar
½ vanilla bean
30 g (1 oz) butter
40 g (1½ oz) plain (all-purpose) flour

To finish
250 g (9 oz) raspberries

For the vanilla ice cream, split the vanilla bean lengthways. Scrape out the seeds and place them, along with the bean, in a saucepan. Add the milk, sugar, egg yolks and salt. Warm over low heat, stirring constantly, until the mixture gradually begins to thicken. Pour the cream into a large bowl and add the hot milk and egg yolk mixture; the cooking process will stop immediately. Mix well and refrigerate for 2–3 hours or overnight. Strain the ice-cream mixture and churn in an ice-cream machine according to the manufacturer's instructions.

For the waffle rolls, in a stand mixer, beat the egg white, salt and both sugars until creamy. Scrape a pinch of the vanilla seeds from the bean and set aside. Melt the butter and allow to cool a little. Fold the butter, flour and remaining vanilla seeds into the egg white mixture. Cover, and refrigerate for at least 1 hour but preferably overnight.

Pour a small amount of batter into a hot waffle iron and cook until you have a very thin waffle. Remove the waffle from the iron, then roll, while still warm, around a chopstick or the handle of a wooden spoon. Repeat with the remaining batter.

In a saucepan, bring the raspberries to the boil with the reserved vanilla seeds and 1 tablespoon water, squashing a few of the berries as you go.

Serve 2–3 tablespoons of vanilla ice cream in small bowls or glasses, then pour over the warm raspberries and serve with the waffle rolls.

RASPBERRY AND CHOCOLATE TART

Chocolate and raspberries really, really like each other!

Pastry	*Chocolate filling*	*Topping*
100 g (3½ oz) cold butter	300 g (10½ oz) bitter dark chocolate	1–2 tablespoons raspberry jam (jelly)
200 g (7 oz) plain (all-purpose) flour,	(at least 70% cocoa)	or Lemon marmalade (page 78)
plus extra for dusting	pinch of salt	250 g (9 oz) raspberries
1 tablespoon icing (confectioners')	pinch of ground cinnamon	1–2 teaspoons honey
sugar	pinch of finely grated orange zest	
pinch of salt	125 g (4½ oz) thickened	
1 egg	(whipping) cream	
splash of milk, as needed	½ teaspoon orange-flavoured liqueur	

Preheat the oven to 180°C (350°F) (conventional). For the pastry, chop the butter into cubes. Place the butter in a large bowl, along with the flour, icing sugar and salt. Using your fingertips, rub the butter into the dry ingredients. Add the egg and knead into a smooth dough, adding milk if the dough is too dry. Roll the pastry out on a lightly floured surface to 3 mm (⅛ in) thick. Line a large pie dish or 4–6 small flan (tart) tins with the pastry and refrigerate for 20 minutes.

Cover the pastry with baking paper, fill with dried beans or baking beads and blind bake on the lowest shelf of the oven for 10–15 minutes. Remove the paper and beans and bake the pastry for a further 10–12 minutes, until the edge begins to turn golden brown. Remove from the oven and allow to cool.

For the chocolate filling, chop the chocolate and place in a bowl with the salt, cinnamon and orange zest. Heat the cream in a small saucepan, then pour it over the chocolate mixture and allow everything to melt together for 2–3 minutes. Stir until smooth, then stir through the liqueur.

Spread the jam over the pie base. Pour over the chocolate cream and leave at room temperature until set. Top with the raspberries and serve drizzled with the honey.

RASPBERRY
SPONGE ROLL

*Fluffy sponge, creamy mascarpone and fresh raspberries will always
be perfect companions! I've baked this dish again and again ever since
I was eight years old. I always make it each year for Mother's Day, except
with strawberries because they are in season.*

Sponge
6 eggs
pinch of salt
50 g (1¾ oz) caster (superfine) sugar
100 g (3½ oz) icing (confectioners')
sugar
150 g (5½ oz/1 cup) plain (all-purpose)
flour, sifted

Cream filling
200 g (7 oz) thickened (whipping) cream
200 g (7 oz) quark
200 g (7 oz) mascarpone
3 tablespoons caster (superfine) sugar
a little finely grated lemon zest
scraped seeds of ½ vanilla bean

To finish
200 g (7 oz) raspberries
icing (confectioners') sugar, for dusting

Preheat the oven to 180°C (350°F) (conventional). Line a square baking tray with
baking paper. For the sponge, separate the eggs. Using a stand mixer fitted with the
whisk attachment, beat the egg whites with the salt and caster sugar to stiff peaks. In
a separate bowl, beat the egg yolks with the icing sugar for 5 minutes until creamy.
Fold the beaten egg white, alternating with the sifted flour, into the egg yolk mixture,
until everything is well combined. Spread the batter onto the prepared tray and
bake for 15–20 minutes. Remove the sponge from the oven and roll up straight away.
Allow to cool.

For the cream filling, whip the cream to stiff peaks. In a bowl, combine the quark
and mascarpone with the sugar, lemon zest and vanilla seeds until smooth, then fold
in the cream.

Carefully unroll the sponge roulade, then spread with the cream and top with the
raspberries. Roll up again and serve dusted with icing sugar.

RASPBERRY VINEGAR

*This vinegar turns salad dressings
into something really special.*

150 g (5½ oz) raspberries
1 litre (34 fl oz/4 cups) apple cider
vinegar

Place the raspberries in a large
sterilised glass jar or bottle. Pour the
vinegar over the top, then seal and
store in a cool, dark place for
2–3 weeks to infuse.

If you like, strain out the raspberries
as soon as they lose their colour.

The vinegar will keep in a cool, dark
place for up to 1 year.

CLASSIC RASPBERRY CAKE

This cake is perfect for summer picnics! You can use any fruit if raspberries aren't available. Try different berries, apricots, plums or rhubarb.

200 g (7 oz) soft butter
200 (7 oz) sugar
scraped seeds of ½ vanilla bean
3 eggs
400 g (14 oz) plain (all-purpose) flour
3 teaspoons baking powder
4 tablespoons milk
250 g (9 oz/2 cups) raspberries

Preheat the oven to 180°C (350°F) (conventional). Line a baking tray with baking paper. In a stand mixer, cream the butter, sugar and vanilla seeds for about 5 minutes. Add the eggs, one at a time, ensuring that each egg is well incorporated before adding the next. Sift the flour and baking powder into a large bowl, then, alternating with the milk, fold into the wet mixture.

Spread the batter onto the prepared tray and scatter over the raspberries. Push some of the raspberries into the batter, then bake for 20–25 minutes, or until a skewer inserted into the cake comes out clean.

Allow to cook in the tray for 10 minutes before transferring to a wire rack to cool completely.

RHUBARB SPRITZ

*Capture the spring, boil it up and
turn it into a summer drink.*

200 ml (7 fl oz) rhubarb syrup (page 202)
40 ml (1¼ fl oz) vermouth
20 ml (¾ fl oz) gin
ice cubes
cold sparkling mineral water or prosecco,
for topping up
rhubarb, to garnish (optional)

Combine the rhubarb syrup, vermouth, gin and ice
cubes in a cocktail shaker and shake well.

Strain into small, well-chilled cocktail glasses, add
1–2 ice cubes per glass and top up with mineral water
or prosecco. If you like, decorate with a strip
of rhubarb or with a piece of the rhubarb cooked
to make the syrup.

SWEET RHUBARB AND STRAWBERRY RISOTTO WITH LEMON BALM

In Austria, we often eat sweet risotto as an afternoon snack in spring.
It tastes best eaten lukewarm or cold.

1 handful pine nuts
1 litre (34 fl oz/4 cups) apple juice
2 tablespoons butter
200 g (7 oz) risotto rice (arborio,
vialone nano or carnaroli)
pinch of salt
60 ml (2 fl oz/¼ cup) orange-
flavoured liqueur
1 teaspoon finely grated lemon zest

2 tablespoons lemon juice
1 vanilla bean
1 cinnamon stick
4 lemon balm sprigs
100 g (3½ oz) rhubarb
100 g (3½ oz) strawberries
2 tablespoons honey
2 tablespoons mascarpone

Toast the pine nuts in a dry frying pan and allow to cool. Heat the apple juice in a small saucepan. Melt the butter in a large saucepan, add the risotto rice and salt, and cook, stirring, for 3–4 minutes until the risotto grains are translucent. Pour in the orange liqueur and add the lemon zest and juice. Split the vanilla bean, scrape out the seeds and add to the rice, along with the bean and the cinnamon stick. Simmer until the liquid has been absorbed. Add a ladleful of hot juice and stir over low heat until the liquid has been absorbed. Repeat until the rice is soft and creamy, about 25–30 minutes.

Pick the lemon balm leaves. Slice the rhubarb and strawberries. Heat the honey in a small saucepan. Add the rhubarb and strawberries, then stir until everything is well coated in the honey and the rhubarb is soft. Fold into the risotto, along with the mascarpone. Scatter over the pine nuts and lemon balm leaves, and serve.

RHUBARB
KETCHUP

*A barbecue on a lazy summer afternoon, in tall grass by a lake, is the perfect foil for
this ketchup. Dipping any kind of barbecued food into my friend Aurelia's magical
rhubarb ketchup always awakens memories for me of good friends.*

1 kg (2 lb 3 oz) rhubarb
1 celery stalk
2 large red onions
1 small piece ginger
1 tablespoon olive oil
1–2 rosemary sprigs
1–2 thyme sprigs
½ cinnamon stick
4 bay leaves

½ teaspoon each of juniper berries,
ground cumin, fennel seeds, coriander
seeds and mustard seeds
50 g (1¾ oz) soft brown sugar
2 tablespoons tomato paste
(concentrated purée)
150 ml (5 fl oz) red wine vinegar
500 g (1 lb 2 oz) tinned peeled tomatoes
salt and freshly ground black pepper,
to taste

Clean the rhubarb and cut, unpeeled, into large pieces. Peel the celery and cut
into pieces. Peel and finely dice the onions. Peel and grate the ginger.

Heat the olive oil in a flameproof casserole dish on the stovetop and sauté the
onion, ginger, herbs and spices over high heat. Add the sugar and caramelise. Add
the celery and rhubarb and cook for 5–10 minutes. Add the tomato paste and cook
briefly, then add the vinegar and tomatoes and stir to loosen the mixture. Simmer
gently for 20–30 minutes, stirring frequently. Season with salt and pepper. Remove
the cinnamon stick and bay leaves, then purée the ketchup thoroughly. To finish,
pass it through a food mill.

Preheat the oven to 100°C (210°F) (conventional). Fill sterilised preserving jars
with the ketchup. Seal tightly and sit in a deep roasting tin or ovenproof dish. Sit
the tin on the middle shelf of the oven, add 2–3 cm (¾–1¼ in) warm water and
poach for 1 hour. Allow to cool, then refrigerate for up to 1 year.

BAKED RHUBARB

Caramelised baked rhubarb, served with yoghurt, quark and semolina or ice cream, is a perfect spring dessert that shines, thanks to its pure simplicity.

500 g (1 lb 2 oz) rhubarb
1 orange
1 vanilla bean
3–4 tablespoons honey
pinch of salt
3 4 cardamom pods
3–4 star anise
1 slice ginger
4–5 fresh or 5–6 dried bay leaves
1 cinnamon stick

Preheat the oven to 200°C (400°F) (conventional). Clean the rhubarb and cut, unpeeled, on the diagonal into short lengths. Thinly peel the orange using a vegetable peeler and squeeze the juice. Split the vanilla bean lengthways. Place the rhubarb in a baking dish and add the orange peel and juice, vanilla bean, honey, salt, cardamom pods, star anise, ginger, bay leaves and cinnamon stick. Mix well, then bake for 15–18 minutes, turning frequently.
Allow the rhubarb to cool before serving.

MILK-BRAISED LEG OF LAMB
WITH RHUBARB AND HAZELNUTS

Even though from a botanical perspective rhubarb is a vegetable, we happily use it in sweet dishes. Savoury rhubarb combinations are rather rare, but here's a recipe I learned to love during an exchange in Altamura, Italy.

1 kg (2 lb 3 oz) leg of lamb
2 teaspoons salt
1 teaspoon sugar
½ teaspoon freshly ground black pepper
6 garlic cloves
5–6 French shallots
1 lemon

1 tablespoon olive oil
1 tablespoon butter
2 sage sprigs
4 rosemary sprigs
2 bay leaves
1 teaspoon fennel pollen (or fennel seeds)
1 teaspoon juniper berries

1 cinnamon stick
1 litre (34 fl oz/4 cups) milk
1 teaspoon cornflour (cornstarch)
400–500 g (14 oz–1 lb 2 oz) rhubarb
1 handful hazelnuts, skins removed

To serve
cooked polenta or fresh bread

Remove the membrane from the lamb and debone, reserving the bones. Rub the salt, sugar and pepper into the meat. Wrap well in plastic wrap and set aside in the fridge overnight.

Preheat the oven to 120°C (250°F) (conventional). Using the heel of your hand, press lightly on the unpeeled garlic cloves. Peel and halve the shallots. Thinly peel the lemon using a vegetable peeler.

Unwrap the lamb and pat dry with paper towel. Heat the olive oil in a flameproof casserole dish on the stovetop. Melt the butter in the dish, then sear the lamb on all sides. Add the bones, garlic, shallot, lemon peel, herbs and spices, and pour in the milk. Transfer to the oven and cook for 2½–3 hours, until tender. If you are short on time, you can cook the lamb at 180°C (350°F) for 1½–2 hours, but the lower the temperature, the more tender the meat will be.

Remove the lamb from the milk and allow the meat to rest for 10 minutes. Strain the milk into a small saucepan. To thicken the sauce, mix the cornflour with a little water until smooth, then add to the milk. Stir and bring to the boil. Clean the rhubarb and slice, unpeeled, on the diagonal. Gently simmer the rhubarb and hazelnuts in the sauce for 10–12 minutes for the flavours to infuse.

Serve the lamb with polenta or fresh bread and the sauce on the side.

STEWED RHUBARB WITH YOGHURT AND ALMOND BRITTLE

Rhubarb stewed with a little orange zest and juice and vanilla is fantastic for breakfast, served with panna cotta or ice cream, or in a crumble. It also goes wonderfully with this almond brittle and a big spoonful of Greek-style yoghurt.

Stewed rhubarb
100 g (3½ oz) sugar
finely grated zest and juice of
1 orange
1 vanilla bean
500 g (1 lb 2 oz) rhubarb

Almond brittle
3 tablespoons sugar
200 g (7 oz) flaked almonds
pinch of salt

To serve
500 g (1 lb 2 oz) Greek-style yoghurt

For the stewed rhubarb, slowly melt the sugar in a saucepan, without stirring, over low heat. Add the orange juice and stir to loosen the melted sugar, then pour in 100 ml (3½ fl oz) water and boil until the sugar dissolves to form a syrup. Split the vanilla bean and add to the syrup with the orange zest. Clean the rhubarb and slice very thinly on the diagonal. Cook the rhubarb in the simmering syrup for 3–4 minutes.

For the almond brittle, melt the sugar in a heavy-based saucepan over low heat. Add the flaked almonds and salt, and stir quickly. Very carefully, pour onto a sheet of baking paper. Place a second sheet of baking paper on top, and roll out to the desired thickness using a rolling pin, making sure not to touch the hot mixture with your hands. Allow to cool, then remove the baking paper and snap the brittle into pieces.

Serve the rhubarb and almond brittle with the yoghurt.

Any leftover syrup goes very well with vanilla ice cream, cakes, crepes or muesli. Combined with prosecco or mineral water it makes a marvellous aperitif (page 195) or a refreshing fruity drink.

RHUBARB CRUMBLE

Fast, simple, wonderful. And the best thing of all? Crumbles always work!

Stewed rhubarb
butter, for greasing
500 g (1 lb 2 oz) rhubarb
finely grated zest and juice of
1 lemon
scraped seeds from ¼ vanilla bean
1 tablespoon soft brown sugar

Crumble
200 g (7 oz) plain (all-purpose) flour
2 tablespoons rolled (porridge) oats
2 tablespoons flaked almonds

2 tablespoons soft brown sugar
pinch of freshly grated nutmeg
pinch of ground cinnamon
pinch of salt
100 g (3½ oz) cold butter

To serve
Greek-style yoghurt or sour cream

Preheat the oven to 180°C (350°F) (conventional). Grease an ovenproof
dish with butter.

Clean the the rhubarb and slice, unpeeled, on the diagonal. In a bowl,
mix the rhubarb with the lemon zest and juice, vanilla seeds and brown
sugar, then transfer to the dish.

For the crumble, combine all the ingredients except the butter in a bowl.
Cut the butter into small cubes and rub into the flour mixture with your
fingertips. Spread the crumble generously over the rhubarb.

Bake for 30–40 minutes, until the crumble is golden and the rhubarb
begins to bubble up at the sides. Remove from the oven and allow to rest
for 20 minutes before serving with yoghurt or sour cream.

PRESERVED RHUBARB

*Preserved rhubarb is crisp, sweet and sour, with
a mild spiciness. It goes particularly well with baked
ricotta (see page 185) or smoked bacon.*

3–4 rhubarb stalks
½ red chilli
2–3 fresh or 3–4 dried bay leaves
1 teaspoon coriander seeds
2 star anise
2 cloves
1 strip lemon zest
200 ml (7 fl oz) red wine vinegar
1 teaspoon salt
1 tablespoon sugar

Clean the rhubarb, cut into pieces on the diagonal and
place in a sterilised preserving jar. Remove the seeds from
the chilli, then thinly slice and add to the jar. Add the bay
leaves, spices and lemon zest. In a saucepan, bring 200 ml
(7 fl oz) water, the vinegar, salt and sugar to the boil and
simmer until the sugar dissolves. Pour over the rhubarb
while still hot and seal tightly. Set aside for 1–2 days in
the fridge for the flavours to develop.

The preserve will keep in the fridge for up to 6 months.

S

STRAWBERRIES

ZANDER FILLET WITH STRAWBERRY AND CAPSICUM SALSA

*The capsicum (bell pepper) works to perfectly harmonise the flavours
of the strawberries and fish in this wonderful dish.*

Salsa
1 red capsicum (bell pepper)
½ French shallot
8–10 strawberries, plus a few whole
baby strawberries to serve
1 handful red sorrel, plus extra
whole leaves to serve
2–3 parsley sprigs
1 tablespoon olive oil
juice of 1 lemon
salt and freshly ground black
pepper, to taste

Fish
1 tablespoon olive oil
1 tablespoon butter
500–600 g (1 lb 2 oz–1 lb 5 oz)
zander fillet
salt and freshly ground black pepper

To serve
strawberry flowers (optional)

Preheat the oven to 200°C (400°F) (conventional). For the salsa, place the capsicum in a roasting tin and roast until the skin turns black. Allow to cool, then remove the skin and seeds and finely dice the flesh. Peel and finely dice the shallot, then finely dice the strawberries. Finely chop the red sorrel and parsley. In a bowl, combine the chopped herbs with the capsicum, shallot and strawberries, then toss with the olive oil, lemon juice, salt and pepper.

For the fish, heat the olive oil and butter in a frying pan over low–medium heat. Cut the zander into 4 portions, then lay, skin side down, in the pan. Season with salt and pepper and gently fry for 3–5 minutes, until the skin is nice and crisp and the flesh is still a little translucent. Baste the fish regularly during cooking with the olive oil and butter mixture.

Serve the fish with the salsa spooned over the top. Garnish with whole baby strawberries, a few sorrel leaves and strawberry flowers, if desired.

STRAWBERRY AND CUCUMBER SALAD
WITH PISTACHIOS, MINT AND YOGHURT

I ate the best strawberries of my life at the Monterey farmers' market in California. The first punnet was quickly devoured, and I will never forget the perfectly ripe, fruity taste. We ate this quick, simple salad with a piece of sourdough bread for lunch, while watching the seals laze about.

500 g (1 lb 2 oz) strawberries
4–5 small Lebanese (short) cucumbers
1 cardamom pod
2 pinches of salt, plus extra to taste
pinch of freshly ground black pepper, plus extra to taste

200 g (7 oz) Greek-style yoghurt
1 teaspoon lemon juice
pinch of sugar
50 g (1¾ oz) shelled pistachios
¼ teaspoon coriander seeds
pinch of pimentón
½ bunch mint

Cut the strawberries into wedges. Slice the cucumbers in half, scoop out the seeds and slice on the diagonal. Using a mortar and pestle, bash the cardamom pod, remove the seeds and finely grind. In a bowl, combine the strawberries, cucumber, ground cardamom seeds and a good pinch of salt and pepper. Set aside for 10 minutes, for the flavours to infuse.

Meanwhile, mix the yoghurt with the lemon juice, sugar and a pinch of salt. Taste, and adjust the seasoning. Toast the pistachios and coriander seeds in a dry frying pan, then roughly grind in a food processor with the pimentón.

Spoon the yoghurt into bowls and top with the strawberry and cucumber salad. Pick the mint leaves and scatter over the salad, along with the pistachios.

CARRIE'S STRAWBERRY PIE

During my time in San Francisco I had the great pleasure of working with and learning from one of the city's best pastry chefs, Carrie Lewis. Ever since then, I've always made strawberry pie and vanilla ice cream at the start of the strawberry season.

Pastry
150 g (5½ oz/1 cup) wholemeal (whole-wheat) flour
150 g (5½ oz/1 cup) plain (all-purpose) flour,
plus extra for dusting
pinch of salt
1 tablespoon caster (superfine) sugar
150 g (5½ oz) cold butter
8–10 tablespoons iced water
1 egg, for brushing

Filling
600 g (1 lb 5 oz) strawberries
55 g (2 oz/¼ cup) caster (superfine) sugar
scraped seeds of ½ vanilla bean
2 tablespoons cornflour (cornstarch)

For the pastry, thoroughly combine the flours, salt and sugar in a bowl. Using your fingertips, quickly rub the butter into the flour, making sure there are still visible pieces of butter in the dough – this is the secret to a crisp base. Add the iced water and shape into a compact ball of dough. Wrap the pastry in plastic wrap and refrigerate for 30 minutes.

Preheat the oven to 180°C (350°F) (conventional). On a well-floured work surface, roll out the pastry, then transfer it to a large pie dish. Cut off any overhanging pieces of pastry.

For the filling, chop the strawberries into small pieces. Place in a bowl and carefully combine with the sugar, vanilla seeds and cornflour.

Fill the pastry-lined dish with the strawberry mixture. Cut small decorations or flowers of different sizes out of the leftover pastry and arrange over the strawberries. Beat the egg and brush over the pastry decoration. Bake the pie for 35–40 minutes until golden brown.

This is best served lukewarm with vanilla ice cream (page 186) or strawberry and vanilla ice cream (page 218).

CHAMOMILE PANNA COTTA
WITH STRAWBERRIES

*Strawberry flowers could almost be mistaken for miniature chamomile
flowers. Perhaps that's why chamomile's aromatic taste
goes so well with strawberries.*

Panna cotta	Strawberries
½ vanilla bean	500 g (1 lb 2 oz) strawberries
300 ml (10 fl oz) thickened	or wild strawberries
(whipping) cream	1 thyme sprig
100 ml (3½ fl oz) milk	2 teaspoons honey
50 g (1¾ oz) caster (superfine)	1 teaspoon Elderflower vinegar
sugar	(page 98) or Raspberry vinegar
1 tablespoon chamomile tea	(page 192)
(whole dried flowers)	½ teaspoon finely grated
3 leaves gelatine	lemon zest

For the panna cotta, split the vanilla bean lengthways and scrape out
the seeds. In a saucepan, gently warm the cream, milk, sugar, vanilla
seeds and bean, then remove from the heat and add the chamomile
tea. Refrigerate overnight for the flavours to infuse. The next day,
strain the liquid and discard the chamomile flowers and vanilla bean.

Soak the gelatine in cold water. Heat the chamomile cream in a small
saucepan, then remove from the heat. Squeeze out the gelatine and
dissolve in the warm milk. Pour the chamomile cream into glasses or
ramekins and refrigerate for about 6 hours, until set.

Halve the strawberries, leaving any smaller fruit whole. Pick the
thyme leaves. In a bowl, combine the honey, vinegar, lemon zest,
thyme leaves and strawberries, then set aside for 10 minutes for the
flavours to infuse.

Serve the panna cotta with the marinated strawberries.

STRAWBERRY AND QUINOA SALAD WITH TARRAGON, SOFT GOAT'S CHEESE AND POACHED EGG

Poached egg with strawberries and quinoa was a dish served to us for breakfast by an old lady at her chicken farm outside Chicago, which doubled as a kitschily decorated guesthouse. Since then, whenever I taste the combination of egg and strawberries, I always think of that lovely lady and her fairytale farm.

150 g (5½ oz) quinoa
500 g (1 lb 2 oz) strawberries
3–4 mint sprigs
3–4 tarragon sprigs
2 tablespoons olive oil
60 ml (2 fl oz / ¼ cup) white-wine vinegar

pinch of finely grated orange zest
juice of 1 orange
4 small eggs
1 handful rocket (arugula), red sorrel or mizuna
salt and freshly ground black pepper, to taste
100 g (3½ oz) soft goat's cheese

Rinse the quinoa under cold water, to wash away any bitterness. Combine 300 ml (10 fl oz) water and ½ teaspoon salt in a saucepan, then cover and bring to the boil. Rain in the quinoa and simmer gently over very low heat for 5 minutes. Remove from the heat and leave, covered, for about 15 minutes to swell up.

Meanwhile, slice the strawberries or chop into wedges. Pick the mint and tarragon leaves and roughly chop. In a bowl, combine the quinoa, olive oil, 1 tablespoon of the white-wine vinegar, and the orange zest and juice.

Fill a saucepan with 2 litres (68 fl oz / 8 cups) water and add the remaining vinegar. Bring to the boil. Break the eggs, one at a time, into a cup, taking care not to break the yolk. Carefully slide the eggs, one at a time, into the bubbling water and spoon the white over the yolk. Reduce the heat – the water should be just under boiling. Cook the eggs for 3–4 minutes then, using a skimmer or slotted spoon, remove the poached eggs from the water and drain on paper towel.

Toss the herbs, salad leaves and strawberries with the quinoa and transfer to a serving plate. Season with salt and pepper, crumble over the goat's cheese and top with the poached eggs.

WILD STRAWBERRIES WITH CREAM
AND CATS' TONGUES

This dish brings back childhood memories of summers we rarely see today.

Cats' tongues
125 g (4½ oz) very soft butter
125 g (4½ oz) icing (confectioners') sugar
125 g (4½ oz) plain (all-purpose) flour
pinch of salt
scraped seeds of ½ vanilla bean
3 egg whites
caster (superfine) sugar, for sprinkling

Strawberries
500 g (1 lb 2 oz) wild strawberries, plus strawberry
flowers to serve
1–2 tablespoons caster (superfine) sugar
scraped seeds of ½ vanilla bean
pinch of salt
100 g (3½ oz) thickened (whipping) cream
1 teaspoon icing (confectioners') sugar

Preheat the oven to 180°C (350°F) (conventional).
For the cats' tongues, beat the butter and icing sugar in
the bowl of a stand mixer until pale and fluffy. Mix in
the flour, salt and vanilla seeds. Gradually add the egg
white until well combined.

Fill a piping bag fitted with a 6–8 mm (¼–⅓ in) nozzle
with the mixture. Line a baking tray with baking paper
and pipe a small dot of the mixture on each corner of
the baking tray to stop the baking paper slipping.

Pipe 10 cm (4 in) long strips of dough on the paper,
leaving a 5 cm (2 in) gap between each strip. Bake the
cats' tongues for 3–4 minutes, until the dough is set,

then sprinkle with a little caster sugar and bake for a
further 5–7 minutes, until golden brown. Repeat until
all the dough is used up.

In a bowl, combine the strawberries with the caster
sugar, vanilla and salt, then marinate for 10 minutes.

Whip the cream with the icing sugar until thick but not
stiff. Divide the strawberries among small bowls and
add 1–2 tablespoons of whipped cream. Garnish with
strawberry flowers and serve with the cats' tongues.

STRAWBERRY AND VANILLA ICE CREAM

*Strawberries and vanilla are always two of the most popular flavours
at the ice-cream parlour, so why not bring them together?*

1 vanilla bean
250 ml (8½ fl oz/1 cup) milk
130 g (4½ oz) caster (superfine) sugar, plus
3 tablespoons extra
6 egg yolks
pinch of salt
500 ml (17 fl oz/2 cups) thickened (whipping) cream
500 g (1 lb 2 oz) strawberries

Split the vanilla beans lengthways and scrape out the seeds. Place
the seeds and bean in a saucepan, along with the milk, sugar, egg
yolks and salt. Heat over low heat, stirring constantly, until the
mixture gradually begins to thicken. Pour the cream into a bowl
and add the warmed milk and egg yolk mixture – this will stop the
cooking process immediately. Mix well and refrigerate for 2–3 hours
or overnight. Pass the mixture through a sieve and churn in an ice-
cream machine according to the manufacturer's instructions.

Preheat the oven to 200°C (400°F) (conventional). Line a baking
tray with baking paper. Halve the strawberries, then place on the
prepared tray and sprinkle over the extra sugar. Bake the strawberries
for 10–15 minutes, until the edges start to turn dark in places. Allow
to cool a little, then finely purée in a blender.

Layer the ice cream and strawberry purée in a container and use
a spoon to mix into a marble pattern. Freeze for 2–3 hours
or overnight.

STRAWBERRY
MILK

This drink brings back such happy memories! Add two or three tablespoons of soaked rolled (porridge) oats for a quick breakfast smoothie. A small banana adds even more creaminess.

---

200 g (7 oz) strawberries
250 ml (8½ fl oz / 1 cup) milk
100 g (3½ oz) yoghurt
pinch of scraped vanilla seeds
1–2 tablespoons maple syrup
sparkling mineral water (optional)

Purée all the ingredients except the mineral water in a blender. Transfer to glasses and top up with sparkling mineral water if you like – it will make the milk even more refreshing.

DRIED FRUIT

STUFFED EGGPLANT
WITH LEMON YOGHURT

A wonderful dish that's particularly perfect for vegetarians. For a vegan variation, substitute the yoghurt for tahini thinned with olive oil and lemon juice. It tastes just as great!

200 g (7 oz) fine burghul (bulgur wheat)
1 teaspoon curry powder
3 tablespoons olive oil, plus extra for drizzling
½ teaspoon salt, plus extra for seasoning
1 red onion
4 small eggplants (aubergines)
(about 250 g/9 oz combined)
100 g (3½ oz) blanched almonds

50 g (1¾ oz) shelled pistachios
150 g (5½ oz) dried apricots
1 small bunch parsley
freshly ground black pepper, to taste
pinch of ground cumin
250 g (9 oz/1 cup) yoghurt
½ teaspoon finely grated lemon zest
mint, to garnish

Place the burghul in a saucepan, along with the curry powder, 1 tablespoon of the olive oil and the salt. Add enough hot water to cover the burghul by about 1 cm (½ in), then stir, cover and leave for 8–10 minutes to absorb the water. Carefully fluff up with a fork.

Peel and finely dice the onion. Heat the remaining olive oil in a frying pan over low heat. Fry the onion, stirring frequently, for 5 minutes.

Preheat the oven to 180°C (350°F) (conventional). Line a roasting tin with baking paper. Halve the eggplants lengthways. Scoop out the flesh using a teaspoon, leaving a 5 mm (¼ in) border. Finely chop the spooned-out flesh, then add to the onion and fry well. Sprinkle the eggplant shells with salt and leave for 10 minutes to draw out excess moisture.

Roughly chop the almonds and pistachios, dice the apricots and chop the parsley leaves and stalks. Add the chopped ingredients to the onion and eggplant and stir well to combine. Remove from the heat and keep warm.

Pat the eggplant shells dry, drizzle with olive oil and place, cut side down, in the prepared roasting tin. Roast for 25–30 minutes.

Mix the burghul with the onion and eggplant mixture and season with salt, pepper and cumin. Drizzle with olive oil, then pack the burghul mixture into the cooked eggplant shells.

Flavour the yoghurt with salt and the lemon zest, and spoon over the eggplants. Serve with a few mint leaves scattered over.

ORECCHIETTE WITH ZUCCHINI, FENNEL, RAISINS AND PINE NUTS

… or 'A summer in Sardinia'.

1 fennel bulb
2 French shallots
1 garlic clove
50 g (1¾ oz) pine nuts
2 tablespoons olive oil
½ teaspoon fennel seeds
finely grated zest of 1 orange
3 tablespoons raisins
1 small zucchini (courgette)

2–3 tablespoons limoncello
200 g (7 oz) ricotta
salt and freshly ground black
pepper, to taste
freshly grated nutmeg, to taste
400 g (14 oz) orecchiette
100 g (3½ oz) pecorino

Shave the fennel into thin strips, reserving the fronds for a garnish. Peel and finely chop the shallots and garlic. Carefully toast the pine nuts in a dry frying pan.

Fry the shallot and garlic in the olive oil. Add the fennel strips, fennel seeds, orange zest and raisins, and fry for 3–4 minutes. Coarsely grate the zucchini, then add to the pan and fry briefly. Add the limoncello and stir through. Remove from the heat, mix in the ricotta and two-thirds of the pine nuts, then season with salt, pepper and nutmeg.

Bring a large saucepan of water to the boil and add 1 teaspoon salt. Cook the orecchiette until al dente, then drain, retaining 60–75 ml (2–2½ fl oz) of the cooking water. Stir the orecchiette and the pasta water through the vegetables, then transfer to serving plates. Finely grate the pecorino over the pasta and scatter with the remaining pine nuts and the reserved fennel fronds.

PORK TERRINE WITH PORK BACK FAT, PISTACHIOS AND PRUNES

This dish might not look particularly beautiful, but don't let that fool you.
Serve it with fresh country bread for a perfect light lunch.

175 g (6 oz) pork back fat, thinly sliced
2 French shallots
1 tablespoon butter
225 ml (7½ fl oz) port
1 egg
1 juniper berry
1 thyme sprig

1 kg (2 lb 3 oz) minced (ground) pork
15 g (½ oz) shelled pistachios, chopped
200 ml (7 fl oz) thickened (whipping) cream
salt and freshly ground black pepper
10–12 prunes
1 pork fillet (tenderloin)
4–5 fresh bay leaves

Preheat the oven to 160°C (320°F) (conventional). Line a 30 × 8 cm (12 × 3¼ in) terrine tin with the pork back fat, so that the fat hangs over the sides of the tin. Peel and finely chop the shallots. Melt the butter in a frying pan, then add the shallot and cook until golden brown. Deglaze the pan with 125 ml (4 fl oz/½ cup) of the port and reduce a little. Lightly beat the egg, crush the juniper berry, and pick the thyme leaves.

In a bowl, combine the minced pork with the shallot and port mixture, the egg, juniper berry, thyme leaves, pistachios and cream. Season with salt and pepper, then knead well. Soak the prunes in the remaining port for 10 minutes.

Spread half the minced pork mixture in the lined terrine tin and sit the pork fillet on top. Cover the pork fillet with the prunes lengthways. Top with the remaining mince mixture. Tap the tin several times to remove any air pockets. Top with the bay leaves, then enclose the terrine with the overhanging back fat slices. Cover with foil or a terrine lid.

Sit the terrine in an ovenproof dish or a roasting tin and add enough warm water to come 2 cm (¾ in) up the sides of the tin. Bake on the middle shelf of the oven for 1½ hours. Remove from the oven, remove the foil or lid and cover with plastic wrap. Weigh down the terrine with a narrow board or a few tins. Refrigerate, covered, for 1–3 days.

Cut into slices to serve. It goes well with crunchy bread and a spring salad with herbs.

BEEF RAGOUT WITH DATES
AND POMEGRANATE

This dish is best enjoyed when the joy of cool and cosy days beckons.

1 kg (2 lb 3 oz) chuck steak
3 tablespoons ras el hanout
2–3 onions
2 garlic cloves
1–2 slices ginger
1 cinnamon stick
salt and freshly ground black pepper
2 tablespoons butter
2 tablespoons olive oil

8 French shallots
2 tablespoons honey
1 pomegranate
200 g (7 oz) dates
2–3 coriander (cilantro) sprigs (optional)

To serve
steamed couscous, burghul (bulgur wheat)
or flatbread

Preheat the oven to 150°C (300°F) (conventional). Heat a flameproof casserole dish on the stovetop. Cut the beef into 3–4 cm (1¼–1½ in) cubes. Rub the ras el hanout into the meat, then add to the dish and fry without oil, until fragrant. Peel and slice the onions. Peel and chop the garlic. Add the onion, garlic, ginger and cinnamon stick to the dish, and season with salt and pepper. Add enough water to almost cover the meat, then cover and transfer to the lowest shelf of the oven for 2–2½ hours to cook slowly.

Heat the butter and olive oil in a frying pan. Peel and halve the shallots, then sauté over very low heat for 10–15 minutes. Add the honey and stir to caramelise the onion. Remove from the heat.

Halve the pomegranate and carefully remove the seeds. Halve the dates and discard the pits. Add the dates, caramelised shallot and half the pomegranate seeds to the ragout 20 minutes before the end of cooking.

Remove the ragout from the oven and discard the ginger slices and cinnamon stick. If you like, scatter finely chopped coriander over the ragout, along with the remaining pomegranate seeds.

Serve with couscous, burghul (bulgur wheat) or flatbread.

THANKSGIVING TURKEY WITH PRUNES AND DRIED FIGS

My Thanksgiving classic, which has been used and refined over many years.

Serves 6–8

Turkey
1 small turkey (about 3 kg/6 lb 10 oz)
1 teaspoon salt

Stuffing
1 red onion
1 tablespoon butter
300 g (10½ oz) sourdough
6 prunes
6 dried figs
½ bunch parsley
200 ml (7 fl oz) milk
50 g (1¾ oz) cooked sweet chestnuts
½ teaspoon finely grated orange zest
1 egg

Glaze
2 tablespoons apricot jam (jelly)
1 teaspoon honey
2 tablespoons soy sauce
120 g (4½ oz) butter

Roasted vegetables
1 butternut pumpkin (winter squash)
500 g (1 lb 2 oz) root vegetables
of your choice
2–3 sprigs each of rosemary and thyme
salt, to taste

Sweet potato mash
700 g (1 lb 9 oz) sweet potatoes
125 g (4½ oz) butter
1 cm (½ in) piece ginger
½ teaspoon finely grated orange zest
juice of 1 orange
300 g (10½ oz) roasting potatoes
about 125 ml (4 fl oz/½ cup) milk
freshly grated nutmeg, to taste
salt and freshly ground black pepper,
to taste

Lingonberry relish
75 g (2¾ oz) sugar
250 g (9 oz) lingonberries or
cranberries
finely grated zest and juice
of 1 orange
160 ml (5½ fl oz) currant juice
pinch of ground allspice
1 cinnamon stick
1 clove

Brussels sprouts
½ teaspoon salt, plus extra to taste
½ teaspoon sugar
250 g (9 oz) brussels sprouts
3 tablespoons butter
1 tablespoon olive oil
finely grated zest of 1 lemon
freshly ground black pepper, to taste

Preheat the oven to 150°C (300°F) (conventional). Wash the turkey, pat dry with paper towel, and lightly salt inside and out.

For the stuffing, peel and finely chop the onion. Melt the butter in a saucepan and sauté the onion. Roughly dice the bread, slice the dried fruit into thin strips, and chop the parsley. In a bowl, combine all the stuffing ingredients and set aside for 20 minutes for the flavours to infuse. Stuff the turkey with the mixture and place it in a roasting tin. Truss the turkey with kitchen twine.

For the glaze, gently warm the ingredients until the butter is melted. Brush the turkey all over with the glaze.

For the roast vegetables, peel the pumpkin, remove the seeds and cut into wedges. Peel the root vegetables, then chop into bite-sized pieces. Place the vegetables in the tin, along with the herbs and season with salt. Roast the turkey and vegetables for 2 hours, regularly brushing the turkey with the glaze and, if necessary, turning the tin to ensure that the meat cooks evenly. If the turkey starts to become too brown, cover the tin with foil.

To finish, increase the oven temperature to 180–200°C (350–400°F) and roast for a further 15 minutes.

For the mash, peel and dice the sweet potatoes, then fry in a little of the butter for 10–15 minutes. Peel and finely grate the ginger. Pour 100 ml (3½ fl oz) water over the sweet potato, add the ginger and orange zest and juice, then cover and boil until the sweet potato is soft. Purée using a handheld blender. Peel and dice the potatoes and boil in salted water for 20 minutes until very soft and almost falling apart. Drain and mash finely using a fork or a potato ricer. Using a whisk, carefully mix the sweet potato purée into the mashed potato. Add the remaining butter and enough milk to make the mash creamy. Season with nutmeg, salt and pepper.

For the relish, caramelise the sugar over low heat. Add the lingonberries, orange zest and juice, currant juice and spices. Bring to the boil and continue to boil for 5–8 minutes. Remove from the heat and set aside.

For the brussels sprouts, bring some water to the boil and add the salt and sugar. Add the brussels sprouts and boil for 5–10 minutes, depending on their size. Drain and plunge into cold water. Halve the sprouts or separate the leaves. Heat the butter and olive oil in a frying pan and toss the sprouts in the pan until just starting to brown. Season with lemon zest, salt and pepper.

Serve the turkey with the roast vegetables, sweet potato mash, brussels sprouts and relish.

PISTACHIO AND BARBERRY
TWISTED LOAF

*Whether it's for breakfast, a mid-afternoon snack or late-afternoon tea – this twist is perfect.
I like to serve it with lashings of butter.*

Dough	Filling	To glaze
200 ml (7 fl oz) milk	150 g (5½ oz) shelled pistachios	2 tablespoons milk
70 g (2½ oz) butter	50 g (1¾ oz) flaked almonds	1 egg
450 g (1 lb) plain (all-purpose) flour,	50 g (1¾ oz) marzipan	
plus extra for dusting	50 g (1¾ oz) caster (superfine) sugar	
25 g (1 oz) fresh yeast	1 teaspoon orange-flavoured liqueur	
80 g (2¾ oz) caster (superfine) sugar	1 teaspoon finely grated lemon zest	
pinch of salt	50 g (1¾ oz) butter	
1 egg	3 tablespoons dried barberries	

Heat the milk in a small saucepan until lukewarm, then add the butter and stir until melted. Place the flour in the bowl of a stand mixer and make a small well in the middle. Crumble in the yeast and mix into the flour with 1 teaspoon of the sugar, 60 ml (2 fl oz/¼ cup) of the lukewarm milk and the salt. Cover, and leave in a warm place for 20 minutes to rise. Add the remaining dough ingredients to the bowl and knead using the dough-hook attachment for 3–5 minutes. Cover the dough again and leave to prove in a warm place for 30–40 minutes.

Meanwhile, for the filling, finely grind the pistachios, almonds, marzipan and sugar in a food processor. Add the orange liqueur and lemon zest and combine. Melt the butter and stir half into the pistachio and almond mixture.

Preheat the oven to 180°C (350°F) (conventional). On a well-floured work surface, roll the dough as thinly as possible, then brush with the remaining melted butter. Spread the pistachio and almond mixture evenly over the dough and scatter over the barberries. Starting at a long side, roll the dough up tightly. Press down well on the roll, then lay on a baking sheet lined with baking paper. Slice the roll lengthways, taking care to leave 3–5 cm (1¼–2 in) uncut at one end. Now twist the two strands together, folding the ends underneath to finish.

Lightly beat the milk with the egg and brush the mixture over the twist. Set the twist aside to rest for 10–20 minutes, then bake for 25–30 minutes until golden brown.

DATE MACAROONS

One of my grandma's many Christmas recipes.
In Austria, we call these date kisses.

4 egg whites
250 g (9 oz) icing (confectioners') sugar
1 tablespoon lemon juice
pinch of salt
100 g (3½ oz) dates
10 g (⅓ oz) cornflour (cornstarch)
200 g (7 oz) slivered almonds
1 teaspoon finely grated orange zest
4 teaspoons orange-flavoured liqueur
100 g (3½ oz) dark chocolate

Preheat the oven to 160°C (320°F) (conventional). Using a stand mixer, beat the egg whites, half the icing sugar, the lemon juice and salt to stiff peaks. Still beating, gradually rain in the remaining sugar, then beat until thick and foamy.

Halve the dates, remove the pits and finely chop. Fold into the meringue, along with the cornflour, almonds, orange zest and liqueur. Using a teaspoon, make small heaps of the mixture on a baking sheet lined with baking paper. Bake for 15–20 minutes, then allow to cool. Melt the chocolate and dip the bottoms of the macaroons into it. Set aside to dry and serve.

MENU SUGGESTIONS

FOR THE LOVE OF YOUR LIFE

Watermelon salad with feta, tomato, mint and cucumber | 136
Nettle and cherry pizza | 67
Strawberry and vanilla ice cream | 218

FOR THOSE WHO ARE ALWAYS THERE

Apple and celery gazpacho with lemon oil | 24
Braised dijon rabbit with blueberries | 51
Peach and pistachio galette | 148

MEMORIES OF CALIFORNIA

Ceviche with grapefruit and lime | 71
Blood orange salad with beetroot and avocado | 68
Zander fillet with strawberry and capsicum salsa | 208
Candied citrus peel (with espresso coffee) | 77

AT THE BEACH

Peaches with burrata, mint and bread chips | 147
*Summer salad baguette with raspberries,
baked ricotta and tea eggs* | 185
Melon

FOR ENTERTAINING FRIENDS

Grilled peach with bacon and ricotta on toast | 144
Chicken korma with apricots and cashew nuts | 29
Lemon pound cake | 72
Fresh fruit

FOR SUMMER HOLIDAYS

Cold apricot soup with fennel | 33
Grilled peach with bacon and ricotta on toast | 144
Port-braised veal cheeks with gooseberries and chanterelles | 115
Currant tart with hazelnut meringue | 80

FOR TREATING YOURSELF

Pulled duck burger with plum sauce | 161
Blackberry cobbler (with vanilla ice cream) | 47

A GERMAN CELEBRATION

Pork terrine with pork back fat, pistachios and prunes | 224
Confit guinea fowl legs with balsamic cherries on cauliflower mash | 61
Raspberry and chocolate tart | 188

MENU SUGGESTIONS

ALFRESCO DINING IN SPRING

Strawberry and cucumber salad with pistachios,
mint and yoghurt | 211
Milk-braised leg of lamb with rhubarb and hazelnuts | 201
Carrie's strawberry pie | 212

HARVEST FESTIVAL

Quince negroni | 178
Thanksgiving turkey with prunes and dried figs | 226
Quince tarte tatin | 174

MEMORIES OF ITALY

Prosciutto and melon | 135
Orecchiette with zucchini, fennel, raisins and pine nuts | 223
Milk-braised leg of lamb with rhubarb and hazelnuts | 201
Cherry tiramisu | 66
Citrus sorbet (drink) | 74

SUNDAY BREAKFAST

Bircher muesli (with seasonal fruits) | 17
or Granola with yoghurt and saffron pears | 154
Strawberry and quinoa salad with tarragon, soft goat's cheese
and poached egg | 215
Cherry (or seasonal fruit) clafoutis | 65

MEMORIES OF SPAIN

Ajo blanco with grapes and grapeseed oil | 122
Quince paste (membrillo) | 180
Sardines stuffed with couscous and apricots | 38
Orange and almond cake | 75

MEMORIES OF SWEDEN

Zander tartare with blueberries, confit egg yolk and crispbread | 56
Venison ragout with elderberries and schupfnudeln | 102
Currant cheesecake | 85

WINTERING IN A MOUNTAIN HUT

Roast pork with apple cider, baked apples and purple potatoes | 26
Date macaroons | 229
Baked apples with vanilla sauce | 18

FOR WATCHING TELEVISION

Potato pancakes with apple sauce | 25

INDEX
A–Z list
────────   ────────

INDEX
Recipe directory

INDEX
Recipe directory

ACKNOWLEDGEMENTS

WITHOUT THE WONDERFUL TEAM
I HAD BY MY SIDE, THIS BOOK
WOULD NEVER HAVE BEEN BORN.

Thanks, Gunda – the best photographer in the world – for your sensitive eye, your feeling for shooting fruit in really unusual light, and the poetry you brought to every single image, letting each one shine like a work of art.

Thanks, Manuela – artist and graphic designer – you captured my taste from the get-go. And you have the best handwriting!

Thanks, Katharina – perfectionist editor and wordsmith – and my very own recipe stylist. You make words sing, and your cooking know-how is worth its weight in gold.

Thanks to my project manager, Stefanie Neuhart, and my publisher, Nikolaus Brandstätter, who immediately recognised how this book's subject was tailor-made for me. Thank you for your trust and your amazing cooperation.

A big thank you also goes to Feigenhof (feigenhof.at), which supplied countless varieties of fresh figs and fragrant leaves.

To Heimo Karner, who shared with me his precious citrus fruit from Schönbrunn Palace in Vienna, and always had time for an informative stroll through his fairytale citrus garden.

Thanks, Jakob and Verena, for supplying seasonal damsons and greengages.

Thanks, Simon, for the secret elderflower walk and the beautiful apple trail.

Thanks, Mama, for the blueberries and wild strawberries you gathered yourself.

Thanks, Javier, from the restaurant Heuer in Karlsplatz, who is now my hero for his last-minute gooseberry rescue. Your garden enriches the whole city of Vienna.

You have made so many pages shine more brightly.

TEAM

BERNADETTE WÖRNDL
Concept, recipes, food styling

GUNDA DITTRICH
Photography

MANUELA TIPPL
Graphic design

KATHARINA WIND
Editing

Bernadette discovered 'food art' while at the Vienna Art School, then gained experience in professional kitchens and spent time in San Francisco working at Chez Panisse. In Vienna, she composed innovative delights and lent new notes to flavours at Babette's Spice and Books for Cooks, a cookbook and spice store. Her profession is hard to describe in words: 'I'm a cookbook author, food stylist, private cook and recipe developer. The focus is always on produce from people who work from the heart and treat nature with respect, sensitivity and vision. Their work creates the essence of good food – only with these ingredients can my recipes taste right.'

Gunda was born in Gnadenwald in the Austrian state of Tyrol. After studying 'graphics' in Vienna, she graduated from studying cultural and social anthropology, majoring in visual anthropology at Vienna University and l'Université Descartes in Paris. She worked in Paris for several years as a freelance photographer and during this time discovered her fondness for still lifes. Gunda's attention to the use of light is particularly important. With her sensitive combinations of set and lighting design, she has developed her own visual language, which has accompanied magazine features and advertisements in numerous publications. She lives and works in Vienna.

Growing up in the Mostviertel quarter of Lower Austria, surrounded by gooseberries, apples and pears, Manuela has also always had an eye for the finer things in life. She studied graphic design and illustration at the New Design Centre in St Pölten, and since 2004 has lived in Vienna working as a freelancer on diverse design projects, and is still a passionate illustrator. In her free time she does pottery, creating minimalistic tableware, and enjoys evenings socialising with friends. She has a special soft spot for laying out cookbooks because they indulge both the eye and the palate. A table coordinated perfectly in terms of food and occasion brings her the greatest joy.

Reading and writing, cooking and eating, travel and discovery – these words describe Katharina's passions. Born in the Lower Rhine region of Germany, she made her way, via studying German and English in Germany and England, to Vienna, to Babette's Spice and Books for Cooks, Austria's only cookbook and spice store. While editing, she likes to cook in her head, in order to recreate, through words, images and smells, the precision and possibilities of each dish. When cooking in real life, she enjoys the freedom to experiment. She has loved the combination of apples and potatoes since childhood: her favourite dish is 'Heaven and Earth' (black pudding, fried onion and mashed potato with apple sauce).

Smith Street Books

First published in 2016 by Christian Brandstätter Verlag as *Obst*
brandstaetterverlag.com

This edition published in 2018 by Smith Street Books
Collingwood, Australia | smithstreetbooks.com

ISBN: 978-1-925418-44-6

Publisher: Paul McNally
Recipes & text: Bernadette Wörndl
Photography: Gunda Dittrich
Illustrations (pp 12–13, 230–231): Shutterstock
Internal designer: Manuela Tippl
Cover designer: Murray Batten
Translator: Nicola Young
Editor (new edition): Lucy Heaver, Tusk studio
Editor (original edition): Katharina Wind

Printed and bound in China by C&C Offset Printing Co., Ltd.

Book 52
10 9 8 7 6 5 4 3 2 1